The Courage To Be
A Stepmom

The Courage To Be A Stepmom

Finding Your Place
Without Losing Yourself

SUE PATTON THOELE

WILDCAT CANYON PRESS
A Division of Circulus Publishing Group, Inc.
Berkeley, California

The Courage to Be a Stepmom: Finding Your Place Without Losing Yourself

Publisher: Julienne Bennett
Editor: Roy M. Carlisle
Copyeditor: Jean Blomquist
Cover design: Eleanor Reagh
Interior Design: Gordon Chun Design
Back Cover Photo: Paige Eden Thoele
Typesetting: Terragraphics, Berkeley, California
Typographic Specifications: Body text set in Sabon 10.5/14.5. Headers are Sabon Bold and Sabon Italic.

Printed in the United States of America

Cataloging-in-Publication Data
Thoele, Sue Patton.
   The courage to be a stepmom : finding your place without losing yourself / by Sue Patton Thoele
       p. cm.
   Includes bibliographical references (p.   ).
   ISBN 1-885171-28-5 (pbk. : alk. paper)
   1. Stepmothers—Psychology. 2. Parenting. 3. Stepfamilies.
   I. Title.
   HQ759.92.T56   1999
   306.874—dc21   98-56160
                                                          CIP

Distributed to the trade by Publishers Group West
10 9 8 7 6 5 4 3 2 1

*With deep love and gratitude to my sons
Mike and Brett Hall, my stepdaughters
Paige Thoele and Lynne Williamson, and
to my husband, Gene Thoele, who
brought us all together.*

Contents

Novice Stepmother

When the idea for this book was first proposed to me, I hesitated. Was I sure I wanted to dredge up all the pain I experienced as a novice stepmother? Wouldn't it be better to leave the memories of tears and turmoil in the past? The process of writing a previous book on marriage had dragged both myself and my husband, Gene, through several hellish knotholes of unfinished business. I wondered if a stepmothering book would reawaken forgotten pain in my now-peaceful relationships with my stepdaughters. Thankfully, that didn't happen. While I *relived* the issues explored in my book on marriage, for the most part I've been able to detach and simply *remember* the hard step-stuff we all experienced struggling to create our new family.

As a novice stepmother I made many mistakes, not the least of which was often sacrificing myself on the altar of I'll-do-anything-to-make-this-marriage-work. It was a Christmas picture of our whole family dressed in clothes representing our extracurricular interests that made something click for me. Gene was in his jogging togs, Mike wore a mask and struck an acting pose, Brett and Lynnie wore their school sports uniforms, and Paige wore her work uniform. Me? I dressed as a maid! Though very apropos at the time, it was definitely a wake-up call to take a look at how I was living my life and managing (or *not* managing) my relationships.

How I wish I'd had a book like this when I married Gene and his girls, but in the early seventies not many people were talking about the realities of remarriage and stepparenting. The only model we had was "the Brady Bunch." Reality was murky and problems hush, hush. So, please know that I am writing this guide from the wonderful wisdom of hindsight, because, in reality, I didn't have more than a tiny clue about how to proceed when I started traveling the stepmother road. My purpose in writing this particular book is very personal. I want to provide the reader with what I *didn't* have as a struggling stepmom, a friendly and experienced hand to hold, the assurance that you're not alone, and a reminder to take care of yourself as well as you do everyone else.

My heartfelt hope and prayer is that *The Courage to Be a Stepmom* will become your friend—a friend that offers you support and encouragement and provides some practical guidelines for making the often rocky stepmother road smoother. I hope that reading it makes you feel better about yourself and gives you permission to let the stepmothering process unfold and evolve. Mainly, I want you to relax a little and absorb a more peaceful way of being a stepmom through reading about my own and other stepmothers' mistakes and successes.

In researching *The Courage to Be a Stepmom*, I interviewed nearly forty stepmothers and found that many of us share the same challenges and joys. Stories are woven throughout the book as examples of both flat-out failure and jobs well done. In reading other stepmothers' stories, their frustrations and solutions, the pits into which they fell and the pinnacles to which they climbed, I hope you will feel less isolated, more connected to the ever growing population of stepmoms, and much more hopeful about the possibilities for love and laughter within your own inherited family.

Of course, there are as many stepfamily scenarios as there are stepfamilies. Yours will be different from mine and, yet, there were common themes in the interviews I conducted. Many of us became too emotionally involved too quickly, knew that we tried to be the mediator (if not the "fixer") in all situations and between all parties, and a good many of us, at least at first, felt the essence of ourselves slipping away under the strain of adjusting to new marriages and new children. *All* of us agreed that the term "blended family" is a euphemism, at least for the first ten or twelve years.

I'm happy and relieved that our stepfamily can now, twenty-five years down the line, sport the term "blended" with ease and honesty. But for many years the phrase merely served as an indictment to what I saw as my failures. Often, simply hearing the term "blended" caused my mind to flash to a picture of my guts being ripped out and tossed in a kitchen blender while some nefarious hand flipped the switch to HIGH.

Though the "blending" process was often difficult, there were also times of joy, pride, hilarity, incredible sweetness, and lighthearted loving in our early years. But my penchant for perfectionism and peacemaking caused me—and I'm sure Gene and the kids also—great discomfort. What I did have going for me in the beginning was my idealism, naivete, and the fact that I was madly and irrevocably in love. Against me were old patterns of guilt, fear, and trying to make everything right for everyone at all times. These challenges to successful stepmothering as well as peace of mind are addressed in depth throughout this book. We'll also look at how we can change the stepmother experience into something more positive not only for us stepmoms but for our families as well.

The six of us who came together lo, these many years ago—at ages 37, 34, 11, 9, 7, and 6—are all adults now. We were honed, shaped, and softened by the stepfamily experience, and I like to think that we're better people for having known, loved, and struggled with each other. I know that I am. I wish the same for you.

I hope also that you can take to heart and into action the advice Margaret, a stepmother to one boy, gave when I asked, "What would you do differently?" She responded, "I'd do what I did, only *sooner*." If my prayers are answered, *The Courage to Be a Stepmom* will help you do what you want and need to do but perhaps a little sooner.

❧

PART ONE

Why Stepmothering Is Difficult

*You hear a lot of dialogue on the death of the
American family. Families aren't dying.
They're merging into big conglomerates.*

—ERMA BOMBECK

Stepmothering can be difficult—a pronouncement, I realize, that may make me eligible for the International Understatement Award. Although a few women I interviewed assured me that stepmothering was an unqualified joy, in fact the easiest part of their marriage, I and the vast majority of other stepmoms, agreed that it was one of the most challenging tasks we had ever undertaken.

When reviewing the preliminary outline for *The Courage to Be a Stepmom,* my editor asked why I wanted to dedicate an entire section to the reasons why stepmothering is difficult. Didn't everyone already know that it was a complex and demanding role? Wouldn't it be better to breeze over the difficulties and get right down to the encouraging stories and "how to's?" The truth is that, although we know intellectually that stepmothering is hard, most of us are ill prepared for exactly *how hard* it can be. We may be incredibly naive simply because we've never had an honest conversation with a stepmother or been close enough to see a stepfamily interrelate. That was certainly true for me. Neither I nor any member of my fledgling family knew any other stepfamilies with whom to talk about the experience. In our circle of acquaintances, we were the only family "conglomerate," as Erma Bombeck puts it, and that isolation made adjusting to each other all the harder.

We are also ill prepared at the advent of creating a new family because the aphrodisiac of new love and idealism courses through our veins. It's rare that we even *want* to be—or can be, for that matter—made totally aware of possible difficulties lurking in the darkened depths of family-merging, and I'm not sure that's all bad. Without a little bit of "love is blind" and the feelings of invincibility that accompany falling in love, we might never have the courage to create families of any kind.

However, I also believe that there is tremendous power in preparation and that it is never too late to be better prepared, no matter where we are in the stepmothering process. It is toward that end that we will honestly explore the often unspoken challenges woven into the stepmothering role.

Even though I will be frank about the difficulties in stepmothering, I think that you will also find encouragement as you read. Comfort can be gleaned from seeing our innermost conflicts written in black and white; it makes us feel less alone and gives us the hope that if *they* can do it, so can we. There were times in the early years of my stepmothering career when I felt as if I were going crazy, and I had no one with whom I could share my feelings. There were scant resources available that laid the realities of stepmothering on the line. So, it was a tremendous relief to me when a friend married a man with two children. At last I could commiserate and compare notes with another stepmother. Talking with her helped me realize that I wasn't crazy. Or, if I was crazy, so was she—and at least I wasn't alone.

If you are in a stepfamily adjustment period right now, you may feel a bit discouraged. If so, I hope that you will find not only solace in the stories about myself and other women who have experienced similar trials but also a better understanding of yourself. Hopefully, the practical tools we have found useful will help make your relationships more peaceful and satisfying. I honestly believe that if I could survive—and eventually thrive—as a stepmom, so can you.

Three Strikes Before You Start

And the trouble is, if you don't risk anything,
you risk even more.

—ERICA JONG

Yes, marrying a man with children is risky. But life is chock full of risks and if we were committed to avoiding them all, we would never leave our homes. In reality, the richness of our lives is often equal to the risks we are courageous enough to take. So, although the risks are high in the stepmother game, it is neither an impossible task nor one without amazing rewards.

But to take those risks and reap the rewards, it helps to know what we face. As I see it, the stepmother role has three strikes against it before the first dinner plate is passed. Those strikes are societal stereotypes (including derogatory language, myths, and fairy tales), the fact that step-relationships are relationships born of loss, and the reality that we are not, and never will be, the *real* mother of our stepchildren. Unlike baseball, these strikes do not mean that we are automatically out of the game or have failed before we started. Far from counting us out, these strikes can actually strengthen us. Learning to understand and work with the strikes against us empowers us to become the stepmoms we want to be.

STRIKE ONE — THE "BUM RAP" OF STEREOTYPES

What adjective first pops into your mind when you hear the word "stepmother"? Wicked, of course. The "wicked stepmother" stereotype is embedded in the very fabric of most cultures, and consequently in our own psyches, even if our personal experience with stepmothers has been positive. Although there are some stepmothers who inflict damage, in my many years as a psychotherapist and confidante, I have heard of only two really wicked stepmothers. The story that stands out in my mind is of a twelve-year-old boy who was visiting his dad and step-mother for a few weeks in the summer. During a collect call to his mother, the stepmother became so angry that she ripped the phone out of the wall, tried to hit the boy with the receiver, and then threw canned goods at the terrified child as he ran out of the house. Pretty dramat-ic. Pretty sick.

While there are a few stepmoms, like the one above, who deserve the wicked label, a vast majority of us sin-cerely want to be loving and supportive to the children in our care, whether they are biological, adopted, or inherited. Even though "nice" greatly outnumbers "wicked," stepmothers still get a bum rap. In the family scenario, their reputation is worse than a mother-in-law's. At least there are mother-in-law jokes, but apparently our society is so brainwashed about heinous stepmothers that we can't even laugh about them.

I am deeply disturbed about the undeserved reputation plaguing stepmothering, because it's a serious concern for more and more women. As of this writing, nearly 40 percent of families living together are stepfamilies. By the year 2000, more people will be living in stepfamilies than in nuclear ones.[1] Instead of shouldering the burden of destructive cultural beliefs, stepmoms and combined families need to be honored, respected, and given the education and support that they need in order to become safe havens for their members. But embedded prejudices die hard. Even though I now consider myself a stepmother emeritus and am secure in my stepdaughters' acceptance, there are burrs still stuck stubbornly under my psyche-saddle. For instance, I inwardly wince when my stepdaughters introduce me as their stepmom—technically correct but culturally damning, and still a bit painful.

I'm continually working on transforming my knee-jerk feelings and believe that all of us involved with functional and fun stepfamilies need to stand on our soap boxes and protest the unfair labels attached to us. The job of merging families is challenging enough without being slathered by the misconceptions that society has long held and that most myths and fairy tales promote.

Flogged by Fairy Tales

As far as stepmothers are concerned, fairy tales could more aptly by called *hairy tales*! Can you name one fairy tale in which the stepmother is a heroine? (Although I can't, I sure can come up with a lengthy list of human stepmothers whom I consider heroic.) Myths aren't much better. While there are a few "good" mythical mothers, there are by far more "bad" mothers and stepmothers.

I'm not an expert in either myth or fairy tale but, like most of us, I was deeply influenced by those I heard or read as a child. As an impressionable eight-year-old, I remember praying feverishly for the safety of a girlfriend who had just acquired—gasp—a stepmother. But, for me, even more disturbing was my anxiety about how stories such as Cinderella and Snow White would impact my little stepdaughters.

There's no getting around it, myths and fairy tales slander stepmothers. In much the same way that the devil is seen as the antichrist and defined as the one who denies or opposes the Christ, stepmothers are viewed as the anti-mother—the one who embodies all the negative emotions we can't comfortably assign to the true mother. Stepmothers are the designated domestic devils, given the odious task of carrying much of our unconscious fear and shadow material. Tagged as a wicked woman, someone to be feared, is it any wonder that we find our role so difficult?

Sticks and Stones
I've never believed the adage "Sticks and stones may break my bones, but words can never harm me,"

because I've been hurt many times by words, and I bet you have also. Therefore, it was very interesting to me to learn that stepfamily terminology is steeped in negativity. For instance, in both Old English and Old High German, the prefix "step" originated in a word meaning "orphan" and was also related to the words "deprive" and "bereave."[2] In *Webster's Third New International Dictionary,* the second definition for stepchild is "one that fails to receive proper care and attention." The definitions for stepmother are "(1) the wife of one's father by a subsequent marriage; (2) one that fails to give proper care and attention; (3) hangnail." Hangnail? Come to think of it, sometimes the stepmothering role, and all the stuff carried with it, is about as welcome as a hangnail. And, as if those origins weren't bad enough, in both Greek and Latin, the noun "stepmother" passed into the general vocabulary as a synonym for "cruel" or "harsh."

It's time for us to reframe and defang the language, especially within our own hearts, and bring "stepmother"—both the word and the person—into the light of reality. She, like most of us, is not a wicked witch. In fact, *real* stepmoms are decent, loving women who yearn to care for their stepchildren and to be a positive influence in their lives. Despite negative societal associations, derogatory language, and toxic fairy tale images, most of the stepmothers I know and have interviewed have not struck out. Out of their intention and desire to love and to care, most mothers-by-marriage find within themselves the ability to nurture and support their inherited children, even when the road gets very rocky. Building any relationship is a continuing process, one that requires gentle patience first with ourselves and then with others. Building step-relationships is no different.

STRIKE 2 — RELATIONSHIPS BORN OF LOSS

Especially when they are young, our own children, as well as the stepchildren we inherit, probably fantasize that their broken homes will somehow be fixed, that Mom and Dad will patch things up, and their families will be together again. (The same fantasy—that somehow their family will be together again—is often present even when it is death, rather than divorce, that has divided a family) Remarriage shatters a child's hope of reunion. As their hope slips away, children often begin a natural grieving process, one they could postpone when there was still a possibility that their parents would reunite. It's important to note that their grieving process sometimes includes trying to destroy a new marriage with the hope that Daddy will see the light and return to Mommie. Knowing that children may attempt sabotage helps keep us from taking their actions and attitudes so personally. It doesn't make it easy, however, merely less personal.

I recently asked Paige, my oldest stepdaughter, if I could have done anything to make it less difficult between us. She replied, "Nope, you were the enemy!"

She was being generous, because I now know there were many things I could have done better if I'd been smarter, older, better prepared, less idealistic, and more secure. But it was enlightening to learn that she'd seen me as the enemy. That, I now know, was part of Paige's grief process. "Enemies" are in a no-win situation where the best course of action is to gently back away and lovingly wait for a cease-fire. That's much easier said than done, and something I regret not being able to do for far too many years.

If your stepchildren's mother is dead, it's very helpful to their grieving process to find age-appropriate ways to help them honor their mother's memory and heal their own sense of pain and loss. Those ways might include a single flower in each child's room on their mother's birthday, visits to the cemetery, counseling with an expert on children's grief, sharing family stories about them and their mother, creating a mother/child picture album, or simply lending a kind and listening ear. When you are attentive to the needs of the children, you will know what to suggest to them or when to elicit suggestions from them. Helping the children honor their mother's memory also helps you gain their trust and love. It's a win-win situation for everyone.

It's important to realize that it isn't only the children who mix grief with the joy of remarriage, or a first marriage that comes equipped with kids. Most of us have ingrained "happily-ever-after" fantasies and, given our heartfelt wish, would opt to marry the perfect man, have the perfect number of children (or a perfect career), and then, years later, doted on by children and grandchildren, happily waltz into our sunset years with this same man. So to be part of a stepfamily means that we, too, must cope with the loss of an old dream or perhaps several dreams.

And in the fresh dreams that arise when we enter a new marriage, we rarely anticipate the ghosts-of-families-past inherited along with stepchildren. Nor do we fantasize about being in relationships born out of loss. But, if you are about to become a stepmother or are currently filling that role, you are gambling that the love you've found and the strength and wisdom that you've acquired will see you through. I'll bet on you. With patience and support, more often than not, we can move through loss and grief and eventually transform rebellious, wounded, and disillusioned people into a happily melded family.

STRIKE 3 — *JUST* A STEPMOTHER

One reality we stepmothers need to keep in mind is that we are not the *real* mother. Even if our stepchildren's mother is dead, drunk, or unfit, *she* remains the real mother, not us. This can be a bitter pill to swallow, especially when you are a stepmom who does most of the mothering and receives very little of the credit.

Happily there are exceptions. There are children who welcome their stepmom with open arms and appreciate her immensely. For instance, thirty-six-year-old Doreen, a dedicated career woman, married Bill, who had custody of his fourteen-year-old son and seven-year-old daughter. After living with her dad and brother for most of her life, Steffi, the little girl, was starved for the affection and attention of a woman. Although Doreen said that she had no idea how to be a mother and felt she floundered around for the better part of two years, Steffi didn't seem to notice. She adored her new stepmom and asked if she could call her Mommy. Hesitant, but willing, Doreen agreed. Because Steffi's real mom was incapacitated by alcoholism and lived in a distant state, Doreen was able to become the mother figure for whom Steffi yearned.

Even in seemingly ideal circumstances, however, you won't be the "real" mother. Laura had been her stepson's nanny before she and his father married. Since she and Jason were very attached to each other, and his real mother was not much interested in him, Laura told me that she fully expected Jason to treat her as a real mom. Instead, much to her surprise, she received the brunt of Jason's resentment about his own mother's casual comings and goings in his life. After being in Laura's home for twelve years, he left to live with his mother. "I was crushed," Laura sighed, "But I understood that he desperately needed his mom's attention and love and felt that he had to try for it one last time."

Different circumstances breed different attitudes and, more often than not, kids are masters at reminding stepmothers of their secondary role. How many of us have had "You're not my *REAL* mother!!!!" yelled or muttered at us? Most stepmoms I know have the not-my-real-mother argument down pat and wisely reply with something accurate and not hurtful like, "I am the mother in *this* house." Intellectually, we know that these are the children of our husband and his former wife or lover. But—and it can be a big but—often our hearts and guts respond as if we were the real mother. Because we often *feel* like a real mom, we can easily fall into several "tender traps" that numb our rational intentions and hook us emotionally as we try to act like the real mother.

Tender Trap #1: Filling a Gap

If we perceive a gap in parenting skill or interest on the part of either of the natural parents, we may feel compelled to rush to the rescue and fill the void. Earth-mother types are especially susceptible to this trap. They yearn to take care of children and make things "all better" for them. But it can be a real setup for pain and frustration.

With tears brimming in her eyes, Sarah recalled that, early in her marriage, she felt she had been asked to take over the role of mother. One day when Sarah was pick-ing up the children, their mother confided that she had never wanted children and had only had them to please her husband and perk up their marriage. She also told Sarah that she had never found the parenting role fulfill-ing or satisfying. "I didn't think I would like it, and I was right," she said. Appalled by this revelation and determined to set it right, stepmom Sarah leaped into the center ring and did everything in her power to become the mother she felt her stepchildren needed and deserved.

Much to her chagrin, neither the children nor their mother appreciated her efforts. Each, in their own way, let her know that she was not the *real* mother and that she should stop trying to act as if she were. "I felt as if cold water was being thrown on my good intentions," Sarah said, "and it took me quite a while to really *get* the message. Before I comprehended that the kids and their mom were telling me to 'back off,' I just doubled my efforts to be the *good* mother and alienated them even more. When I finally got the message, I was crushed, because I really had been doing what I thought I'd been asked to do and what seemed best for everyone, including the kids' mom. Boy, was I mistaken!"

Another poignant story that underscores the power of the mother-child bond came from Georgia whose step-daughter, Cory, had been estranged from her natural mother for over ten years. Georgia willingly took on the roles of both mother and mentor. However, when Cory became seriously ill (and eventually died in her mid-thirties), she only wanted her real mother, not the woman who had nurtured her for more than a decade. Georgia admitted that, even though she understood Cory's feelings, she felt hurt.

Georgia's experience is a valuable lesson for all stepmoms. The fact is that no matter how wonderful we are, no matter how much we add to our stepchildren's lives, and no matter how much they love us, in most cases, blood is thicker than remarriage.

Tender Trap #2: All Children are Created Equal

Another trap is the "fairness trap." We want all the children to feel loved and accepted. We feel we should treat them equally and without favoritism. We're right about that, but kids are really good at playing the fairness card to their own advantage and, consequently, they often *take* advantage. It's in no one's best interest when children wield too much power.

If we have children of our own who live with us full time and our husband's children visit, we may bend over backwards to be fair and "make it up" to our husband because he sees his children less. In fact, we may try to "make it up" no matter what the living arrangements are. Therefore, it's wise to check up on ourselves. Are we trying to play "real mom" to all the kids in order to be fair? If so, is it working for us and the kids? Do the kids misuse or abuse our desire for fairness? As a dyed-in-the-wool pragmatist, I encourage you to continue doing whatever is working. But I also encourage you to be honest about what isn't working. In the interest of peace, it's easy to overcompensate or appease to the detriment of our sanity, the kids' sense of security, and the family structure.

Tender Trap #3: Our Heartfelt Desires for the Children to Be Ours

The most tender trap of all is our desire for the children to be *our own*. Maybe we yearn to share the intimacy of parenthood with our husbands, maybe we are absolutely crazy about these particular kids, or maybe we're like the "Old Woman in the Shoe" and the more kids the better. Whatever the reason, if in our heart of hearts we yearn to be the real mother, it's easy to act as if it were so and doing so can set us up for bouts of heartache.

In rare cases acting "as if" works. Louise had one son when she married a man with three sons and a daughter. After much trauma and turmoil, her stepdaughter went to live with her mother but the boys all stayed. "From the day my stepdaughter moved out, I considered myself the real mother of all the boys." After a moment's pause, she added, "Maybe it was the only way I could cope with two extra kids." With the boys, it worked. With the daughter, it didn't.

Usually the stepmother role is more like Patricia's. Her stepdaughter was only five when they first met and Patricia told me, "I remember exactly where I was when I noticed the phrase 'I want to raise this little girl!' running through my mind." Patricia's attachment was three-fold. Her teenage son was living with his dad; she had always wanted a daughter; and the little girl was both spoiled and ignored by her biological parents. Aware that she wanted to be Karen's real mom, Patricia took care of herself by slowly shifting gears. "I became a shape-shifter," she told me. When queried about what that meant to her, she answered. "I tried to figure out what form I needed to take in order to be as supportive as possible to both Karen and myself. Sometimes that means I'm very active and sometimes it means that I back off."

Tender Trap #4: Legalese

As unfair as it may be, stepmoms have no legal rights or privileges and, often, no official standing even when they are the "active" mother. Between clenched teeth, Nicki told me about the frustrations in attempting to care for her live-in stepson. "It was a bear wrestling with schools and medical personnel because I, as a stepmother, had no rights to insure immediate care or do any decision making for this boy! Even though *I* was doing all the parenting, his dad had to be in on every decision. He wasn't even an interested dad. One day it took me several frustrating hours to track him down to get permission for his son to have stitches. When I got hold of him, you know what he said? 'Whatever.' I had been sweating bullets over this kid's well-being and the official parent says, 'Whatever.'" It's no surprise that Nicki and Whatever are no longer married.

Because officialdom does not recognize stepparents, it's very important to find out your state's policies about obtaining crucial and immediate medical treatment for a stepchild. In some states, a limited power of attorney signed by your spouse allows you to act in case of emergency. For your own safety and sense of well-being, it is wise to ask your attorney to draft the appropriate forms.

Nullifying The Three Strikes

By becoming more aware of the three strikes against stepmothers, we can neutralize their destructiveness. With preparation and realistic expectations—not to mention generous dollops of self-love, compassion, and forgiveness—we stepmoms can make a huge difference in shaping our own families and supporting future stepfamilies. Educated and aware stepmoms (and stepdads) can help change today's reported staggering 60 percent divorce rate among remarriages with children and create loving, functional, and fun combined families.[3]

From my experience, I know such families are possible when approached with patience and perseverance.

And I've talked to countless stepmothers who have created powerfully healing and nurturing homes for themselves and their "his-hers-and-ours" kids. Thankfully, stepfamilies have been in existence long enough to realize that they can't always "go it alone" and are creating crutches, comforters, and criteria to help them weave their families together with as few nicks and scars as possible. The great news is that more and more excellent resources in terms of books and organizations are becoming available for stepfamilies.

A Wild Ride

We tend to think of the rational as a higher order,
but it is the emotional that marks our lives.
One often learns more from ten days of agony
than from ten years of contentment.

–MERLE SHAIN

A brand-new stepmom with no children of her own lamented, "I just need someone to tell me that I'm not nuts and that it really *is* possible to take this chaotic mess and create a peaceful family from it." I murmured some encouraging words and, after drying her eyes, she said softly, "This is the hardest thing I've ever done. It's a wild ride!" Yep, that it is—but it is also a journey of learning. You are actually, as Merle Shain, author of *Some Men Are More Perfect Than Others,* assures us, learning a tremendous amount as you experience the agonies of stepmothering emotions. And that learning, though you may not always know how, can become a gift and a grace.

A ROLLER COASTER OF EMOTIONS

Chances are we will be disappointed if we expect our stepfamilies to be calm and peaceful most of the time.

Families are made up of people. People are often in pain. People may be angry and unsure of themselves. People sometimes have no compunction about splattering their feelings wherever they can and on whomever they encounter. And some people may see their stepmom as a logical target. But, because stepmothers are also human, we often become less than calm and reasonable ourselves.

Although I'm not proud to report this, I remember telling my rebellious teenage stepdaughter (the one who once considered me "the enemy"), "I am so angry with you right now that I would love to throw you through this window." Thankfully, neither of us remembers the rest of the encounter. I do know that I didn't throw her, but the scary thing was that I was so upset, I *could* have.

It's not always possible to stay off the emotional roller coaster and censor or control our feelings, but it *is* possible to control our actions and make wise choices about how we express our feelings. Looking back, I'm not sorry that I let Paige know how I felt, but I am also forever thankful that I made the choice not to act out those feelings. It is to our credit that both of us controlled ourselves.

Almost all the stepmothers I interviewed talked about the profusion—and confusion—of feelings that accompanied their role. The unpredictability of their emotions surprised many women, and even the most easygoing admitted to wrestling with jealousy, resentment, anger, confusion, grief, joy, exhaustion, frustration, pride, shame, guilt, excitement, and insecurity. While there are positive emotions attached to stepmothering, those that brand our hearts and cause the wildest rides are the most difficult ones and, consequently, the ones we like to talk about when given the chance.

One great statement concerning the depth of our stepmother emotions came from Janice, a seasoned stepmom, who laughingly said, "Hell, I felt crazier as a new stepmother than I did during my little sojourn in the loony bin." She wasn't kidding. Before marrying her husband and his kids, Janice had experienced a nervous breakdown and been hospitalized briefly. "All this step-stuff was so confusing," she continued. "There were so many more people in my house and each of them had feelings of their own, and those feeling were always *changing*. The nerve of the buggers!" Her sense of humor and being able to laugh with her husband were the major factors in their surviving the upheaval of early stepparenting, Janice says.

Be assured that, at one time or another, *everyone* in a combined family tippy-toes around in an emotional minefield. There are days when no one in a stepfamily knows what to do, how to handle their feelings, or how to relate to these people who have been forced on them by circumstance and not by choice.

As a generalization of the destructive ways with which we try to cope, men in our culture are taught to stuff their feelings and project blame onto others. They are likely to react by saying, "If I'm sad, upset, inconvenienced, or angry, it must be *your* fault." On the opposite side of the cultural coin, women are trained to internalize blame, take too much responsibility for everyone, and strive for peace and perfection. They may respond to finger pointing by questioning themselves, "Maybe all his feelings *are* my fault. Maybe I did goad him into this reaction." Continually accepting blame and second guessing ourselves can lead to depression and/or resentment.

It is important to remember that we don't act in negative ways because we're horrible people; we do it because we're *vulnerable* people unsure how to constructively and cooperatively create a viable family-by-marriage. Because we are so vulnerable, it is immensely important that we have absolute compassion for ourselves and other family members in the difficult experiences we share. When compassion is too difficult to feel, we can still hold in our hearts the intention to feel compassionate as soon as humanly possible. If God is aware of our step-struggles, I'm sure She/He will understand and applaud our intention and hopefully someday help make our intention a reality.

PET ROUTINES, PATTERNS, AND PROJECTIONS

When I asked what advice they would give to other step-moms, a frequent response of veteran stepmothers was,

"You've got to be flexible!" Amen. When we say yes to intermingling our family—or just ourselves—with his family, we also say yes to the challenge of becoming more flexible about our pet routines. By agreeing to increase our flexibility quotient, we are also—albeit often times unwittingly—saying yes to changing patterns that may be deeply ingrained and assenting to taking responsibility for our own projections while learning to dodge projections aimed at us. If that sounds daunting, it is. But, because of the power that lies in routines, patterns and projections, it's also an unparalleled opportunity for growth and honing our souls.

The Power of Pet Routines

Many of us derive comfort, stability, and joy from our favorite routines. Pet routines or habits may actually act as a steadying rudder in the tumultuous seas of hectic, daily life. Is it any wonder, then, that disruptions in our routines cause such anxiety? Because they are so precious to us and healthy for us, we need to be exceedingly gentle with ourselves as daily, seasonal, and special routines are interfered with, rearranged, and changed.

Some of my favorite routines are holiday ones. I love holidays. When my sons were very young, I had my holiday routines down pat. Whether we went to my husband's family, my family, or stayed at home, I indulged in my pet practices and loved every one of them. But then—wham, bam, thank you ma'am—a divorce shattered those cozy routines and stained the holidays with loss and sadness. The first few holidays that I spent without my children were among the most excruciating times I've ever struggled through. Although other family members and friends were helpful and concerned, nothing could replace sharing those precious, lost routines with my boys.

Eventually, I was able to find the energy and desire to create new routines based on whether I had my boys with me or was alone. But that energy and desire did not magically spring forth one day. Not at all. Being able to create new and nurturing routines came as a result of much tender loving care from friends, personal therapy in which I did intense inner work on my own sense of worthiness, countless conversations with others, and through the grace of God.

When the boys and I teamed up with Gene and the girls, the term "holiday routine" became even more of an oxymoron. In theory, all four children were to alternate holidays with their other parent. In reality, special circumstances often came into play and the idea of alternating holidays went out the window. To this day, holidays occasionally include none of the kids, often involve some of them, and sometimes we all get to be together. Most of the time we can adapt and have a fun-filled and sacred time wherever we are, but, honestly—for me, at least— there is still a little empty space in my heart for each child who is absent on a holiday. That little hole-in-the-heart is present for most moms and stepmoms when they are away from those they love on holidays, no matter what the reasons. Yet, hard as it is, we can learn to be flexible.

Flexibility is not only necessary when planning holidays and special occasions but also is essential for the small daily routines, In fact, we can sometimes be more gracious about altering the "big" routines than we can be when watching our treasured small routines go down the drain.

"I had trained my kids to get themselves ready for school and quietly go about their morning business while I drank my coffee and read the paper," Belle sighed. "But my husband's kids can't seem to understand that they need to leave me in peace in the morning." With a bigger sigh, "I miss that quiet morning time more than anything else." Eventually, Belle will probably be able to teach her stepchildren to honor her morning routine, but until that time, she is definitely learning to become more flexible. In the interim, she gives herself permission to disappear to a coffee shop alone on mornings when she has had enough.

Diana is another stepmom who found the disruption of daily routines very difficult. She and her only son, Andy, had established a relatively quiet and serene routine in their four years alone together. "I picked him up after school, we chatted on the way home, ate dinner together, and then went our separate ways—my son to his homework, the telephone, and sometimes television, and I did whatever needed doing. *And*," she stressed, "we both loved the house to be quiet and orderly." Not so with her new husband and his three kids. They liked loud music and roughhousing, and they thought that dirty towels were meant to decorate the floor.

As you can well imagine, Diana and Andy found it difficult to respond to the loss of their peace and order with either flexibility or equanimity. In fact, it took several months of therapy before their combined family came up with solutions that addressed each person's needs and preferences adequately—not perfectly, but enough so that each felt everyone had compromised equally.

This particular family's solutions included a list of cleanup chores that had to be done before the children left for school, a no-trespassing rule for Andy's room, and headsets for anyone listening to music. Solutions that work for your family may resemble these, but they may also be entirely different. Your challenge is to find what works for *you*.

Of course, our set routines are interrupted more often when we live in the same house with our stepchildren. If they visit, we can often grin and bear the disruptions and maybe even welcome having set routines rattled around a bit. It actually can be fun and enlivening to get "outta the groove" once in a while. But the truth is that you'll probably find your flexibility quotient challenged—at least a tiny amount—each and every day of the stepfamily journey. As we realize that such challenges are a natural and normal part of the step experience, it's easier to relax into increased inner and outer flexibility.

The Power of Patterns

Contributing heavily to the wild ride of stepmothering are the old patterns of behavior and belief that everyone brings into a new family relationship. These patterns spring from our family of origin, the society in which we live, previous relationships, and as a response to unhealed wounds and insecurities left unaddressed. But for the sake of ourselves and our new family, we need to recognize our old patterns and deal with them in constructive ways.

One of the patterns that I brought with me into my new family was established years before when I was a teenager and was trained to acquiesce to boys in order to be popular. As if it were scalded into my thirteen-year-old psyche, I can remember the exact place we were when my mother first talked with me about the requirements of dating. Always acquiescing seem phoney and felt uncomfortable, but, at the time, the idea of being a social outcast was even more formidable to me than losing myself. I'm sorry to say that I became no more adept at honestly speaking my truth in my first marriage than I had been in high school. As a result, more of my self was buried under layers of insecurity and fear.

By the time I met Gene, I had learned a lot from being a single parent and going to graduate school, and I was firmly convinced that I had the right to speak out and be listened to with respect. Rationally, I knew that we needed to be equal partners in our marriage, but my imbedded-in-the-gut fear of rejection kept me returning to my early pattern of acquiescence. Consequently, I had a terrible time "getting real" with Gene and insisting that he pay attention to the issues that I brought up.

And Gene, raised in a patriarchal German tradition, carried the pattern that the father was the unquestioned head of the household and his word was law. Even though Gene believed in equality and wanted a life *partner*, it was still difficult for him to overcome the pattern of supremacy learned at his father's—and society's— knee. Without a doubt, these two out-dated and destructive patterns have tripped us up more than any others. But they have also provided rich and rewarding growth opportunities from which we've both benefited.

Because you, your husband, and the children are human and all have a past, you will naturally drag old patterns of behavior and belief into the new family situation. Many of these patterns will need tempering and some will require outright exorcising. Because dealing with these patterns is often one of the most difficult aspects of creating a family, I find it helpful to think of old patterns as free weights. As we have the courage to lift, heave, and grapple with them—or sometimes lay them aside—we will gain immeasurable strength, wisdom, and maturity.

With awareness, intention, and desire, we can alter many long-term patterns by ourselves or with the help of our partner and/or children. Tackling the past, dealing with the present, and moving into the future is facilitated when we are consistently gentle with ourselves and other family members. As we seek to change patterns that no longer nurture our growth and happiness, we need to support ourselves and each other with unqualified acceptance and unshakable hope. Sometimes, as we deal with particularly difficult or destructive patterns, we will need to support ourselves with the objective guidance of a therapist or wise friend. Such loving support makes it easier for us all to dig out from under the old and embrace the new.

The Power of Projections

Projection is a difficult and complex psychological process. In general, projection occurs when we attribute our own ideas, feelings, or attitudes to other people. The habit of projection can be incredibly damaging to relationships when we try to lay blame, guilt, or responsibility on another person as a way of coping with our own fear or anxiety.

Anything that is unrecognized, unresolved, wounded, or disowned within us is likely to be projected onto another person or situation. What we do not see within ourselves, we have a tendency to project onto another person as if it were their flaw, foible, or fault. When unwilling or unable to become aware of our own uncomfortable or shameful feelings and beliefs, we unconsciously identify some "other" to carry them for us. This other person then becomes the "bad guy" about whom we can be righteously indignant.

Kick-the-dog stories are examples of projection. Because you can't kick your boss, who is the real focus of your anger, you lash out at something or someone more accessible, like the dog. If we don't want to recognize our wish that our stepkids would (at least sometimes) evaporate, we may scream at them, ignore them, or label them incorrigible, while continually seething with resentment. Or we may lash out at their father or withdraw in silence. Owning our own projections means we realize that it is resentment and anger within ourselves that we are projecting onto the children or their dad. We do this, perhaps, because it's just too hard for us to believe we can be, or at least feel, so unloving or angry. Even if the kids are being difficult and your anger is justified, everyone will be better off when you can acknowledge your own feelings, take back your projections, and deal with the situation honestly. Only through recognizing your own feelings can you transform them.

A typical stepfamily scenario occurs when the kids can't "fix" their natural family and make it the way it was. Overwhelmed by frustration and sadness, they project their feelings of anger, impotence, or guilt onto you, the "wicked stepmother." Their real target may be their natural parents, but acknowledging that may simply be too scary or feel too disloyal to the kids. Because they are not attached to you, you make a wonderful target.

As an example, Annie caught the brunt of her three stepdaughters' grief and resentment toward their biological mother. "All the girls were needy and resentful," she said. "Their mother rejected them and they resented *me*!" The girls are now women and understand that they blamed the wrong mother, but that was what they needed to do at the time in order to preserve their belief that their own mother cared for them. Luckily Annie, who was fifty when she inherited the girls, was an older and wiser stepmom than many of us. But, even though she understood the concept of projection, it still hurt.

We're all human and vulnerable, so of course it hurts. Therefore, when faced with unstoppable projection, I advocate The Armadillo Approach: Stand up for yourself, but also grow a shell and slowly move out of the way.

The Armadillo Approach is especially important for the stepmothers of girls. Girls, more often than boys, equate liking their stepmother with disloyalty to their real mother. And, because of the fierce loyalty girls have for their mothers, they can be extremely wounding with their projections toward their stepmoms.

Fiona, a deeply caring stepmom, looked at me with soulful brown eyes and said, "It took about ten years for my stepdaughter to relate to me as the woman I really was. She was so ticked at her mother for having a time-consuming career and equally ticked at her father for loving me, that she concocted a fantasy stepmother, a real low-down bitch." With a sigh—I notice that many stepmothers sigh—she continued, "It took me quite a while, a lot of reassurance from my husband, and some therapy to really believe I *wasn't* the woman she thought I was. We have a tight relationship now, but it couldn't happen until she realized that I was a handy stand-in for the real objects of her sadness and anger."

While girls, by nature of gender and competition over their fathers, often project emotions onto their step-mothers, boys also have unresolved feelings they project. Darla, whose children and stepchildren are now grown, shared a poignant conversation that she had with her son Matt. He was eleven when Darla moved with Matt and his brother to another state to marry a man she'd met on vacation. Matt explained his defiant behavior toward his stepfather by saying, "I felt abandoned by you and was so miserable and scared at being jerked away from everything I knew and loved! And I was mad as hell about being away from Dad. I was not about to like the dude who, in my mind, was the cause of all my misery! I wanted him to be miserable too, and I was just the person who could do it."

Now in his thirties, Matt is able to verbalize his earlier pain and explain the need to project it outward. As a preteen, however, he had neither the knowledge or experience to understand that spewing venom on his stepfather was counterproductive to his own happiness and created great upheaval in the newly forming family. Luckily, as adults, Matt and his mother were able to explore how they both felt in those difficult years and, through a series of conversations, came to a better understanding of each other and, therefore, felt more deeply connected.

No family member is immune to playing the projection game and, because men are often trained to be detached from their feelings, they can make excellent projectors. I remember a morning when Gene angrily accused me of not caring about his girls because I had let them go out to play with the boys before anyone had eaten breakfast. Although stung by his anger, I realized that his comment probably didn't have much to do with me, since I was stirring pancake batter at the time. To this day, I don't know—and neither does he—what was going on inside him. Maybe he felt guilty, maybe he was sad, maybe he was actually angry at me for something else and couldn't express it.

Another less mysterious projection came from Rose's husband. Continually he complained that she was overindulgent with her adult children and allowed them to exhaust and deplete her. As an excellent psychotherapist who felt neither exhausted nor depleted, Rose recognized the projection for what it was and gently questioned her husband about his own feelings. Eventually he was able to admit that he felt jealous about the time she spent with her children. When she knew that a need for more attention was the real cause of his anger, Rose was able to respond in ways that satisfied each of them.

Owning Our Own Projections

Projection damages all relationships because it doesn't honestly address the real feelings and issues and, therefore, makes it impossible to examine and work through the true causes of dissatisfaction and pain. Probably one of the best things we can do to insure the success of our marriage and our relationships with our stepchildren is to own our own emotional projections and teach other members of the family to own theirs also. Doing so allows us to recognize, heal, and accept the places within us that need to be loved. Not owning our own projections means that we will continue aiming our unexamined feelings at others and thwart intimacy in the process.

Please give yourself the priceless gift of exploring and acknowledging your own feelings in order to diminish the possibility of projecting them onto others. Very importantly, don't allow yourself to be another person's target. Being able to dodge unfair projections is very empowering and keeps us from feeling victimized. Sometimes, simply stepping out of the way permits feelings to boomerang back to the one who is projecting and gives them the opportunity to own their own feelings and subsequently express them honestly and constructively.

Healing and accepting ourselves enables us to better love our families, extended families, and friends whereas projecting our unresolved "stuff" onto others creates chasms between us. It is connection, not chasms, that we desire with those we love.

TEACHERS OF LOVE AND CONNECTION

Some of our greatest emotional pain is the result of feeling abandoned, unloved, and misunderstood by our mates. Many stepmoms echo the same idea: "The hardest part is not feeling connected to my husband," "If only we were able to work together as a team, things would be so much easier," or "Loving and honest communication was often nonexistent, and that made everything a thousand times more difficult."

Stepmothers who feel supported and loved, those who manage to forge strong bonds of communication and have deep, enduring friendships with their husbands, all feel that every stepfamily challenge and heartache is worth it. Why? Simply because they "are in it together," because they "enjoy and count on each other."

Only two stepmoms I spoke with maintained it was their husbands who taught them how to be more loving and honest. Their husbands insisted on open and honest communication at all times. In my experience, however, women are often more adept in the relationship arena than men. Therefore, teaching love, connection, and constructive communication regularly rests squarely on the stepmother's shoulders. Such was the case in my own family.

Women seem to have the intuitive knowledge that heart connection is the essential ingredient our souls long for in all of our relationships, especially those with our lovers, husbands, and children. And, most know how to create such connection. Because we are naturally and culturally attuned to the nuances of relationship, we women continually need to access our wisdom concerning heartful connections. We are asked to accept the challenge of becoming the teachers of relationship, the guides for love and connection.

I am passionately committed to the belief that, as women, our great mission and sacred task is to create a climate in which heart energy—love, compassion, inclusion, intuition, acceptance, and tolerance—can come into balance and harmony with mind energy. And I haven't met a woman yet who doesn't yearn for the intimacy that heart to heart connection fosters. In order to survive and thrive, we, our children, our marriages, and our very planet need to bask in the energy of love, equality, caring, and respect in relationships of all kinds.

Believe me, I know that this responsibility sometimes feels like a giant burden and that it's tempting to resist being the relationship teachers. That's okay, as long as we eventually come back to an acceptance that right or wrong, fair or unfair, it's just the way it usually is. A few weeks ago I spoke with a new stepmom named Joelle who was discouraged about her relationship with her husband. "Do I *have* to be his teacher?" she asked. "Is he ever going to teach *me* something about connection and intimacy?" She wasn't thrilled when I answered, "Probably not in ways you're hoping for. The reality is that women are usually the tutors as far as love and relating goes, but he has many other valuable things to teach you."

I shared with Joelle some of the ways that Gene and I have been each other's teachers through the years and told her that I, too, felt rebellious and discouraged at times. However, our family works better and more naturally when I accept that, in the intimate relationship arena, I am the one who knows more innately how to do it. Something must have rung true for Joelle, because I recently saw her and she stated cheerfully, "I'm just in there teachin' away, big time!"

Let no one tell you otherwise: creating a new family that includes stepmothering *is* a "wild ride." We may occasionally lose our grip on our emotions and tumble head over heels into our own anger and woundedness.

That's okay. At times we will find ourselves living out old patterns and projecting our unacknowledged darkness onto both ourselves and others. That's okay too. We're all human. The trick is to learn from it all.

When something has gone less than perfectly, pick yourself up (asking for help when you need it), figure out what happened and own your part of it, make amends if necessary, allow yourself to heal, and bless yourself with acceptance. Having the courage to gather up our mantle of wisdom after a fall, settle it firmly on our shoulders, take a deep breath, and once more accept the challenge of being teachers of love and connection is an incredible gift we can give to both ourselves and our families.

PART TWO

❧❦❧

Making Stepmothering Manageable And Enjoyable

Keep breathing.
–SOPHIE TUCKER

A dear stepmother friend of mine, who has dealt with many challenges throughout her life, once told me, "I sometimes say to myself 'This is a day to breathe in and out, nothing more. Just breathe in and out and wait for tomorrow to come.'" There are days during our stepmothering adventures when we would do well to take her wise and simple advice. Just breathe and wait. This, too, shall pass. And it behooves us to pay attention and enjoy on the good days, for they, too, shall pass.

Of course, we breathe all the time, but when we consciously deepen our breath—especially during times of stress and upset—we literally bring more ballast and balance into our bodies, emotions, and spirits. Interestingly, the words breathe and spirit are closely related and many spiritual traditions—including the Christian tradition—teach that The Divine breathes life into women and men. By breathing deeply, we become more spacious and draw on a strength larger than our own.

When I'm feeling fragmented or off center, I find it very helpful to sit on the floor or the ground, and imagine that I'm drawing my breath from the very center of Mother Earth and allowing her to anchor me firmly in my body. If I'm looking for inspiration or want to tap into my intuition, I alternate between drawing breath from the core of the earth and imagining that my breath is coming into my body through the top of my head—from the heart of God or the Cosmos.

As you well know, we need both balance and ballast in order to manage and enjoy stepmothering. Even though it sounds deceptively simple, try the breathing idea the next time you feel off center. Merely breathe deeply, in and out, and imagine your breath anchoring you to the very core of Mother Earth. I think you'll find it helpful. Breathing—just simply breathing—is a good starting point for making stepmothering manageable and enjoyable.

Taming The Expectation Tiger

*It's astonishing in this world how things don't turn out
at all the way you expect them to!*

—AGATHA CHRISTIE

I like to call unrealistic expectations "Expectation Tigers," because they are predators that devour our peace of mind. Expectation Tigers lurk behind every tree along the stepfamily path. Seductively they whisper within us, "Since we love each other so deeply, we'll surely love each other's children and everyone will always get along wonderfully with everyone else. Our love for each other will be strong enough, wise enough, and artful enough to solve all problems effortlessly. We will be the exception to all the horror stories about stepfamiles that people love to share. We will live happily ever after."

While most of us are much too educated and psychologically sophisticated to voice these fantasies, even to ourselves, they live on nonetheless. Hidden deeply within our psyches is the programming that, not only *can* we live happily ever after but it is *our* job to make that happen for everyone.

Along with the feeling that we must make sure everyone is happy comes our determination to disprove the bad press stepmothers get. We will not be wicked. We will be patient and unfailingly understanding, willingly setting aside our own needs to unconditionally care for children whom we may not love or even know very well. Impossible? Yes. But when our natural inclination to do it all and do it well teams up with our desire to immediately be the perfect stepmother, it leads to crippling expectations of ourselves as well as of our current and acquired families.

Much better than impaling ourselves and our families on the sharp claws of unrealistic expectations is learning to relax into the process of *becoming* a cohesive unit. A great way to begin relaxing is to debunk the fallacy that there is such a thing as an instant family and to accept the reality that forging a stepfamily takes time.

THE FALLACY OF THE INSTANT FAMILY

Love at first sight is every bit as rare in stepfamilies as it is in the dating world. As a once-burned, pretty darned practical woman, I scoffed at the idea of love at first sight until it happened to me. Gene and I fell in love the first night we met. But neither of us fell immediately head over heels for each other's children. They grew on us—sometimes like barnacles, I confess.

Gene's first barnacle encounter came earlier in our relationship than planned. I had just moved to Hawaii and the two of us were squeezed into an efficiency apartment for a month or so before we could move to our rental house. It was to be a fun, albeit cramped, pre-honeymoon before my sons, Mike and Brett, joined us at the end of the summer. When the boys' father called to say that he needed to send them to me earlier—two days from now—I panicked. But Gene assured me that he was looking forward to having the boys in his life and we would manage.

A couple of days later, two bedraggled, air-sick, tightly-wound, apprehensive boys arrived in Hawaii. Without going into all the gory details, suffice it to say that within two weeks, eleven-year-old Mike had casts on both arms, one wrist broken as a result of a fight with his brother and the other one from riding his bike in a forbidden parking garage. Nine-year-old Brett was hyperactive and badly sunburned, and Gene was equally fried—not from the sun but from the unaccustomed pandemonium. Then one day, I stepped from the shower, looked out our tenth floor window and saw my two precious boys inching along the ledge around the top of the five-story parking garage while battling intense trade winds. Thankfully Gene wasn't home to see a nude, hysterical mother leaning out of a very high window screaming like a banshee at her overly adventurous boys! As a family, we've laughed a lot over that misadventure, but it certainly wasn't funny at the time.

Our premature togetherness under less than ideal circumstances catapulted Gene from his fantasy about having stepsons into the reality of the difference between boys and girls. Although he was unfailingly kind to the boys, he withdrew from me into the shadows of an oh-my-god-what-have-I-done-now turmoil. Who could blame him? The boys were thrust into a difficult situation, acting out, and pushing the boundaries as kids are prone to do. I was a nervous wreck who spent many a night curled up on the bathroom floor crying. An inauspicious start, but definitely one that dispelled the myth of the instant family. Or at least suspended it for a little while.

Adjustment Is Gradual

Therapists and researchers are discovering that it takes between five and seven years for a stepfamily to blend into their own unique semblance of family. Mine took longer, and our slow start can be chalked up to two reasons. First, I tried too hard and expected too much too soon. Second, it took us about six years to have everyone under one roof for an entire school year. During the first five years, Gene's girls lived with us full time for only one year, although we generally saw them several times during the week. My boys were gone each summer and Mike lived with his dad the same year that the girls came to live with us full time. This all seems so convoluted that I'm reminded of the old song, "I'm My Own Grandpa."

During our five years in Hawaii, we never had all four kids as full-time residents at the same time. When we moved to California during the fifth year of our marriage, Mike, Brett, and Lynnie came with us, but Paige didn't join us for a few months. As you can imagine, *flexible* was a concept with which we became well acquainted!

Only after we were in the same house, in a new town where Gene and I were the primary parents, did we begin to coalesce into a family unit. Even then, one of the kids resolutely refused to participate as an engaged and cooperative family member due to unresolved pain and confusion.

Interestingly, the children accepted each other as siblings long before the family actually felt like a real family to us adults. Of course, we had flashes of feeling connected, but our ability to stay connected to and complement each other grew with time, and continues to do so. Most of the time our intertwined relationships are rich and rewarding for each of us.

Emulate Kids and Cats: Ooze in Gently

Even though we know better, some adults secretly expect—or cross their fingers and hope—that the two families will immediately and magically blend into one. Much wiser and more realistic, children usually adjust differently. Unless they are extremely needy, kids tend to wait and cautiously sniff out the situation. Consciously or unconsciously, they are checking to see if there is a safe place for them in the stepfamily: Am I going to be okay? Will Dad or Mom still love and take care of me?

Do I like this new person and, if there are new 'siblings,' their kids?" Sometimes children push the boundaries and act out their pain in very creative ways, usually testing the waters, wondering, "Let's see if they will still hang out with me if I do this or that."

While acting-out behavior is best left to the kids, we responsible adults in a family-by-marriage would be wise to emulate their cautious behavior by going slowly, acquainting ourselves with the new situation, studying the people, and eventually finding our appropriate place. It's a lesson I learned the hard way.

Probably my main regret is that I didn't go slowly and stand back with Gene's girls, Lynnie and Paige. After we were ensconced in our house and somewhat settled, I leaped in with both feet, hoping and dreaming that the six of us would miraculously intermingle into a Hawaiian facsimile of the Brady Bunch. When that expectation didn't materialize immediately, I felt like a failure and redoubled my efforts, which was absolutely the worst thing I could have done. Unrealistically expecting everyone to behave like a happy, supportive family led to tension, rebellion, and disappointment, and it interfered with the natural bonding process that could have taken place, given the chance. (After writing this paragraph, I caught myself heaving a big sigh and thinking, "Live and learn.")

Had I been better prepared and more secure as a young wife, mom, and stepmother, I could have more easily understood where everybody was coming from, kids and new couple alike. Although Gene and I had chosen each other, the kids had not chosen the upheaval that our marriage brought into their lives. His girls didn't even meet me until I was already living with their dad, and my boys were uprooted from California to Hawaii, twenty-one hundred miles from their father, their school, and the only home they had ever known. We're lucky and blessed to have outlasted the chaos and to eventually have become a cohesive and fun-loving family.

I was not alone in my trying-to-be-too-much-too-soon early stepmothering. "My husband paid through the nose to get free and marry me," Heather explained. "I wanted desperately to please him, be the perfect wife, and make his kids so happy that he wouldn't regret being with me. But, unfortunately, my overenthusiasm really turned the kids off." Whether our attempts at instant family intimacy spring from idealism, ignorance, or the need to please, the results are usually the same. Our actions push the kids away, make us feel like failures, and expose our hearts to an all out attack from the Expectation Tigers.

Of course, there are a few wise women who do it well right off the bat. They either know intuitively how to ooze into stepmothering gently and easily or have been given priceless guidance about doing so. Jane, a mother of two with a ready laugh and quick smile, is a great example. Preceding her marriage to a man who had a son and daughter, she and her therapist explored ways in which she might make the adjustment period easier for everyone. "My therapist had been a stepmother, so she was a jewel," Jane grinned. "First, she helped me let go of my fears and preconceived ideas about what I needed to do and what we, as a family, needed to be. Then we came up with the idea of using the same principles for introducing the kids into the family that you use with a new kitten or cat. Lovingly let 'em alone and let them sniff out their new home. And," she laughed, "keep 'em away from the other cats in the house for a little while."

She continued, "On the first day of a long-term visit from my husband's children, I took my kids on an overnight excursion so that Jim and his kids could get reacquainted, settle in, and check out the joint without us as distractions. It was great, because the next day Jim's kids were actually glad to see mine. I still stayed in the background, provided food, talked only a little. Now *that* was the hard part!" she confessed laughing. "When Jim's kids came to us full time the next year, I still left 'em basically alone, unless they came to me. The hardest part was backing off and letting Jim discipline his kids, because I'm an in-your-face kinda gal, but it turned out to be worth it."

Remembering our cat, Max, adjusting to our home, I could see the wisdom in the kitten/cat approach to integrating ourselves and other family members into step situations. Although Max had been extremely affectionate in the animal shelter's visiting room, he stayed behind the dryer for the first three days after we brought him home. We provided food, a little music, sometimes sat in the laundry room and read, and occasionally chatted with him. But basically we lovingly let him alone, as Jane did her stepkids. It worked for them and it worked for Max.

Even though this definitely falls into the do-what-I-say-and-not-what-I-did category, I want to suggest to all stepmoms, new and seasoned alike, that it's never too late to stepmother more constructively. First, erase any erroneous beliefs about having an instant family and embrace, instead, the reality that creating a family circle takes time—sometimes lots of time. Ooze in gently. Let the kids set the pace. Wait, nurture, water, fertilize, listen closely, set reasonable limits, wait some more, and allow the family to bloom in its own way and in its own time. Pray, and be patient with everyone—especially yourself.

An Unnatural Alliance

A natural alliance is formed when a couple gets married for the first time—even if a baby is on the way—and they have at least a few months to adjust to each other before accommodating to the needs of the child that they created together. Two of the biggest challenges for stepfamilies are that you don't have an initial period of alone time and the children are not yours and your husband's. When you give birth to a child, or adopt or take in foster children, both parents are in it together. Whether it's a joint decision or a joint surprise, you share a unified vision with your mate. New stepfamilies form an unnatural alliance of *your* kids and *my* kids.

Most often stepchildren enter our lives post-cuteness and after the wonderfully seductive stage of dependent babyhood has passed. While it's natural to bond with a tiny, helpless infant or a terribly cute toddler, having only anecdotal awareness of an older stepchild's history makes bonding with them a much longer and more conscious process. Expecting more is unrealistic and can sabotage the formation of a natural alliance.

Lacking sweet baby memories or a bonding history of any kind, it's no wonder that committing to the children and beginning to think of them as *ours* is difficult, especially when they resent and resist us. It takes time, shared experiences, and constructive decisions. Also remember that, while we may grow to think of the kids as ours, they may never think of us as *theirs*. A soul-polishing paradox to be sure.

Personally, I think that the prescribed five-to-seven-year adjustment period is an optimistically low number when we are speaking of creating new family traditions and patterns or becoming loyal and supportive step-relatives. History is not immediate, and a shared history is a major factor in creating the intimacy and accountability found in bonded families. Making and sharing a history with other persons involves knowing them, establishing minute connections with them, learning their idiosyncrasies, protecting their vulnerabilities, appreciating their humor, understanding how they respond under pressure, listening to how they feel, and offering unlimited hugs when needed.

Accepting the unnatural alliance into which they have been thrust and being willing to create new family bonds is easier when children feel they have a say in the matter. When a stepmom has known the kids or been a friend of the family, children may readily accept her new role as dad's lover/wife. Mary, for example, had known the family of her much older lover for many years, and they had been circumspect about their sexual relationship. But on one family trip, the time seemed right and she casually asked the kids, "Do you mind if I bunk with Poppa tonight?" Hardly looking up from their game, permission was granted. If, however, a child had responded negatively, Mary and her lover would have remained in separate bedrooms.

Now I'm going to leap to the other side of that issue and say that, although it's great when kids can feel included in their parents' decisions, it is by no means healthy for kids to have unlimited control. One woman tearfully told me that she had broken her engagement to the love of her life because his nine-year-old daughter treated her so poorly. She knew that marriage would only exacerbate the problem since her lover was unwilling to discipline his daughter. She canceled their wedding, and both adults were—and still are—heartbroken. That is too much power for any child to wield.

Adult Children—Advocates or Adversaries?

The older our beloved's children are when we marry, the easier it is to resist the fallacy of the instant family. Perhaps it's because we, too, are older, wiser, and more experienced. Or perhaps it is because older kids and adult children generally don't share our daily lives and we are not responsible for them in the ways we are for younger children. We can also meet teens and adult children as equals and speak frankly with each about what our relationship is and is not.

However, just because everyone is older doesn't mean that things will automatically be peachy keen. Adult children are often warm and welcoming and delighted about their father's happiness with you, but they can also be wounded and rebellious or spoiled and inconsiderate. Lucy's adult stepson was very concerned that his inheritance had vanished when his father married her. On visits to their home, he was surly, slovenly, and rude. Feeling guilty at being an absent dad during his son's formative years, Lucy's husband was not willing to confront his son. Being an understanding but forthright woman, Lucy solved the situation herself. On one visit, she took her stepson, Sam, aside and addressed his fears, point-blank. After a period of denial, Sam acknowledged his feelings. From that base of honesty, they could really talk and come to a clearer understanding. "I told him," Lucy said, "that he was welcome in my home at anytime as long as he acted like a reasonable and responsible guest when he was here. No more rudeness and no more waiting on him."

Being a resolved stepmother, Lucy totally ignored Sam on a subsequent visit when his behavior remained unchanged. "Within two days, he became the sweetest young man and has been a welcome house guest ever since. I've grown to like him very much," Lucy said, smiling.

No matter what our stepfamily circumstances, ideas about living happily ever after as an instant family are best labeled "fiction" and filed accordingly. As we become better educated about the fact and fiction associated with combined families, we will begin to tame the Expectation Tigers and live relatively happily some, if not most, of the time with some, if not most, of the people.

The Challenge of Extended Families and Ex Spouses

Our parents are often woven into our happily-ever-after fantasies through our expectation that, as a result of our marriage, they will be overjoyed to have more grandchildren. Realistically, our parents may not give a toot about more kids and may never actually get well acquainted with our stepchildren unless we all live close to each other. Since few of us live down the street from our parents anymore, it's unusual for stepgrandkids and stepgrandparents to have the opportunity to spend much bonding time together.

Such realities don't seem to deter our expectations, however, a revelation I gleaned from my interviews with stepmoms. Many expressed sadness over their own parents' disinterest in their stepgrandchildren. In contrast, only one women was disappointed that her husband's parents didn't accept her children. Since I don't believe that parents of women are less accepting than parents of men, I have no explanation for that discrepancy unless, perhaps, we tend to expect more of our own parents. Since these stepmothers had committed to their husband's children, many automatically expected that their parents would follow suit.

Sharon's disappointing experience is a case in point. She was only thirty when she married forty-eight-year-old Ben who had four children, ages eleven to eighteen. Although Sharon's mother lives close by and these are the only grandchildren she will ever have, she steadfastly refuses to include them and is tactless and sharp in their presence. "I was so disappointed in the entire extended family's reaction to these kids, some of whom lived with me, and all of whom I saw as my only chance to experience the mother role. But Mother was, and is, the worst. Her behavior is abominable. It has driven a wedge between us and makes holidays very hard," Sharon lamented.

Pam is another stepmom whose parents remained indifferent to her two stepchildren. However, dealing with her husband's feelings about the issue was more difficult than dealing with her own. His children were seven and nine when Chet and Pam were married. He became increasingly hurt and angry as he realized that his in-laws were never going to bestow upon his kids either equal attention or inheritance. In order to have a more harmonious marriage, Pam and Chet eventually agreed not to talk about her folks.

I, too, experienced difficulty with family. When first introduced to me, my future mother-in-law turned her back and walked away without acknowledging the introduction. I understood that her actions were motivated by a deep belief that Gene's divorce was morally wrong, but it still hurt. Happily, the rest of Gene's family was immediately welcoming. Actually, my boys won my mother-in-law over. Never had they been more charming and sweet than when they first met her. As a mother of boys herself, she apparently decided that I must be all right to have such cute kids.

Ex Spouses

The "ex" stuff can be very destructive. Consequently, if we find ourselves stuck in the web of obsession-with-an-ex, we need to free ourselves immediately. Obsessing with the past haunts developing relationships and taints the energy and vitality they need to thrive. Judith and her new husband, J.D., spent a majority of their conversation time chewing on real and imagined wrongs committed by

J.D.'s ex-wife. Tiring of the subject, Judith asked a friend for advice. "Don't engage in conversation on that subject," her friend advised. "Drop your end of the conversation rope."

The next several times J.D. brought up the subject of his ex-wife, Judith responded, "I'm sorry your feeling so bad about this, but it's not a subject I want to discuss." or "I can tell this is really hard for you, but I think it's between you and her, not you and me." In a short while, Judith was excited to note that J.D. rarely brought his ex-woes up and their conversations became much more interesting and their life together more satisfying.

If you need to talk through issues with your ex, it's best for both you and your husband to do it with someone other than each other. As much as possible, in your relationship together, let the past be the past and concentrate on the present. Negativity—especially about exes—drains us of vital life-forces that are best poured into our marriage and stepparenting.

The fact is that parenthood and stepparenthood are vocations meant to be undertaken by grownups. Unfortunately, ex's—and I am including all of the parents of all of the children involved—often resort to childish and immature behavior, sometimes plopping their children smack dab in a war zone of hostility, recrimination, blaming, and backbiting. I have only a few soap boxes upon which I resolutely stand, and here's one of them. If you or any of the adults dealing with the children are not able to get along with each other, it's time to get help. The children are suffering as a result of your conflicts.

To a woman, every stepmother urged, "Get help. Go to therapy," or "Join a group," when problems with exes catch kids in the cross fire. One, a therapist herself, listed the following reasons why a stepparenting group was helpful to her; 1) I gained perspective, could begin to see the bigger picture rather than drowning in my own little problem puddle. It widened and deepened my view; 2) It broke the isolation I was feeling; 3) I got feedback about how I could act and respond more positively; 4) The best part, for me, was watching the dads wake up to the reality of what was really happening in their own families.

If your husband's former wife is hard to deal with, back off and let him handle as many situations as possible. Their relationship is neither your business nor responsibility. If your ex is difficult, try to take care of the difficulties yourself. However, you and your present husband do need to deal with the impact former relationships have on your marriage. Sorting out that emotional tangle is often impossible without the help of an objective observer such as a counselor, trusted friend, clergyperson, or group.

When there is turmoil in the extended family, do what you can to support the children in the best way you know how. If they are willing, you might have them draw pictures showing how they feel when Mommie and Daddy fight. You might offer an non-judgmental listening ear (realizing that, before doing so, you may have to hop in your car and scream your lungs out), or suggest the kids be given the gift of therapy so that an uninvolved adult can provide the support and awareness that they need. Most kids desperately need to know that all of this pain and upheaval is not *their* fault.

Because it is so easy to get stuck at the point of our greatest pain—and divorce or a relationship break-up may, indeed, be the source of our most intense anguish—realistically we often cannot heal alone. To break the patterns and heal the wounds, we may need the help of a compassionate and well qualified professional. Please, if your life is haunted by the fallout from old relationship wounds, give yourself (and your children) the gift of therapy.

So, you never know in stepfamilies. Maybe the in-laws will be outlaws and ignore the kids, or maybe the kids will be the catalyst for helping our parents accept a situation that they wish didn't exist at all. Sometimes everyone gets along fine, and no one has unrealistic expectations or disappointments to contend with. No matter what the particular situation, our former spouses and extended families often give us ample opportunity to keep our expectations fluid, including the expectation that we can and should be in control.

Letting Go of Control

Another stepmom, Trish, and I were laughing over the fact that, early in our stepping careers, we actually believed we could control each and every situation. With great glee she shared what her husband said after a particularly chaotic encounter with all five kids: "This damned stepparenting stuff is like being in a rubber raft with no paddles!" Trish added, "Finally we just decided to give up control and hold on for the long haul!"

If you are having trouble holding on right now, take heart from the couple in the rubber raft. Even though they were well aware of the complications of stepping before they married, they still encountered rapids and white water where they needed to hang on for dear life. "I actually learned to yield control from the stepparenting groups that I led," Trish shared. "After hearing countless stories of control gone awry, I got the message."

We may be fully aware that our peace of mind diminishes in direct proportion to the number of things we feel we *must* control, and yet we may still not be able to loosen our grip and let control slip away. If that's the case for you, please treat yourself gently and remember that all of our control issues raise their shaggy little subconscious heads in unfamiliar situations or during stressful times. When you find yourself clinging desperately to your ideas about how things *should* be, ask yourself, "What am I afraid of right now?" and "Why and where am I struggling for power?"

In reality, whether we are control freaks or consummately easygoing, our jaws will occasionally be clenched as a result of parenting—step or otherwise—because kids are messy and unpredictable. When I told Gene that I was working on the "Why Stepmothering Is Difficult" section of this book, he grinned and said, "Because it includes children?"

Because stepmothering does include children, it's a good idea to give up the expectation of control. The more relaxed we are and the more we "don't sweat the small stuff," the better off we'll be. Giving up control doesn't mean that we knuckle under and become a victim of either circumstances or other people (our children included). Of course there need to be rules and guidelines in families, but the fewer the better. Once we realize that control arises out of fear whereas caring guidance arises out of love, we can commit ourselves to letting go of control. With practice, we will find that it's both empowering and peaceful to give up control and to learn to go with the flow of love.

REASONABLE AND REALISTIC EXPECTATIONS

We've looked at some of the unrealistic expectations we bring to the stepping experience. But as stepmoms, what reasonable and realistic expectations can we hold in our hearts? We can expect the stepmothering journey to be paradoxical: trying and rewarding, confusing and calming, traumatic and loving, enraging and soul stretching.

Pencil in Imperfection

As we live out the paradox of the stepmothering journey, we need always to remember that perfection ain't possible. All of us will act out our frustrations and unresolved pain in hurtful ways: all of us will respond inappropriately on occasion; each of us will give in to unrealistic expectations; some of us may lose control and do or say things about which we will feel tremendous remorse. Rebellion and rule-breaking may reign during various stages of each child's development, and we stepmoms may watch ourselves become someone we never wanted to be.

Life is so much easier when we can give up unrealistic ideas about how things *should* be and matter-of-factly pencil imperfection into our agenda. Better yet, use ink! For many years I penciled in imperfection by having an index card on the fridge that read, "No one said it would be easy!" Knowing that imperfection is a natural part of the stepmothering adventure makes it easier to be gentle, compassionate, and forgiving with all members of the family, including ourselves.

Love Me, Be Kind To My Kids

"Love me, love my kids" is not a reasonable expectation of ourselves or our men. However, because the well-being of our children is a primary responsibility and a heartfelt desire, what are the realistic expectations of us adults regarding the children?

Veteran stepmother, Cheryl stated it well, "I told my new husband, 'My kids are a huge part of me. When you are kind and supportive to them, it is loving to me.'" With a twinkle, she added, "He said, 'Ditto.'" For Cheryl and her husband, kindness and concern for each others' children has grown to include loving them dearly. Although not an initial expectation, love has blossomed as a welcome bonus.

It's reasonable to expect—and even insist—our partner treat our kids with kindness. If kindness is not forthcoming or our partner mistreats the children in any way, as their mother, it is our mission to protect and support them in whatever ways necessary.

Relaxing into the reality that things will be different than we think they will be and often different than we *wish* they were, allows us to create a climate of acceptance in which our stepfamilies can evolve naturally and lovingly into the best families they can be.

Taking It One "Step" At A Time

As for accomplishments,
I just did what I had to do as things came along.

—ELEANOR ROOSEVELT

As with most of life's paths, the stepmothering path has many twists and turns. Because of the bends and curves, it's impossible for us to see too far down the road. Age-old wisdom assures us that the journey of a thousand miles begins with one step. As stepmothers, it's important to remember that our journey not only begins with one step but also continues a single step at a time.

Each small, cautious, and thoughtful step allows us to carefully place the foundation stones of the family structure we are building. In my own haste to create a wonderful stepfamily edifice, I rushed in where angels feared to tread, slinging building blocks hither and yon. No wonder the kids often ducked and ran for cover.

Luckily, mistakes make the best teachers. And, happily, mistakes can also be rectified. Of course we can't change the past, but we can learn to understand why we made particular mistakes, change our behavior in the present, and apologize for past errors. In fact, our ability to say, "I was wrong and I'm sorry. What I did or said was not kind or constructive. I apologize and hope it didn't hurt you too much" helps create trust, understanding, and safety in relationships. Such "fessing up" also provides an excellent model for honesty, and gives kids the freedom to admit to and atone for their own mistakes.

One wonderful bonus that I've received from writing *The Courage to Be a Stepmom* is increased openness and an ability to honestly reminisce with all four of our "kids." (No matter how old they are, they'll always be kids to us.) It is a blessing—one that's brought greater understanding and closeness—to look back now, with the wisdom of hindsight, and explore what we were feeling then in a difficult and confusing situation. In addition, I feel forgiven and understood concerning my early years of "stepmuddling."

ANTIDOTES FOR STEPMUDDLING

My own "muddle through" stepmothering history has yielded a few "short-steps" that I hope will help make your step-enterprises more manageable and enjoyable.

Short-step # 1 — Step Back

Especially during the first months or years of your relationship, let your stepchildren's dad take care of anything and everything that he's willing to do for them: discipline, driving, discussions, dinner, whatever.

As much as possible, let the kids make the first moves toward you. Wait for them to invite you into their lives and hearts. This doesn't mean that you don't engage them in conversation and activities, but it does mean that you let go of expectations about how they should feel toward you—and how you should feel about them.

Cultivate an observer persona, a part of yourself that can be compassionately detached like the android, Commander Data, on *Star Trek: The Next Generation*. "Hmmm...fascinating," he might murmur during times that would be strange and stressful to mere humans. When we step back and simply observe what's going on, circumstances often do transform from infuriating to fascinating.

It's never too late to step back. Years into our marriage, I finally gained the wisdom to step back from one of Gene's girls. That belated move has paid off in a relationship with which we are both pleased and comfortable.

Short-step # 2 — Step Aside

If you are the primary caretaker of your stepchildren and/or your own children, it is loving and polite to step aside when their other parent visits. When the stepchildren are older, it may be thoughtful of you to step aside during weddings and other events where all parents are present. If you have doubts about what your stepchildren are comfortable with in any given situation, ask them, and adhere to their wishes. Even though stepmothers have no designated role in family celebrations, such as weddings, we can get creative about our participation and contributions. Suzanne's stepdaughter felt torn between hurting her mother's feelings and honoring her bond with Suzanne while planning her wedding. They agreed that Suzanne would quietly make the bridesmaids' gifts and be available to talk about the wedding details. At the wedding itself, Suzanne stepped aside and remained in the background.

Short-step # 3 — Step Forward

If we, or any of the children, are being physically or emotionally hurt, we need to step forward to protect and defend whomever needs it. In the case of spousal or child abuse, it's essential to get yourself and the children to a safe place where you can receive the assistance and guidance that you deserve and need. In extreme cases, you may need to gather up the courage and confidence to step forward into a whole new life.

Thankfully, most of us will need to step forward for less dramatic and drastic reasons than abuse. We may need to step forward to share our feelings, nurture ourselves and others, provide guidance and counsel, or make our wants and needs clear without judging or casting blame.

Short-step # 4 — Step Down

When I was a kid, my mother sometimes said, "Get down off your high horse, Sue!" when I was being particularly bossy or know-it-all. If you find yourself thinking you know how everything *should* be or how everyone else *should* act or feel, step down from your high horse. Dismounting isn't easy to do, says I, the recovering know-it-all, but it is one of the major ways to build a successful partnership with your spouse and all of the children.

Short-step # 5 — Step Up and Put Your Foot Down

There are times in all relationships when you need to put your foot down and say, "This is nonnegotiable." There are some rules that cannot be broken, some behavior that is always inappropriate, and some limits that will not stretch. For me, one nonnegotiable is respect. I firmly believe that each family member deserves respect. A second is noise—the kids were only allowed to listen to music through earphones when I was within earshot. Only you know what your own nonnegotiables are. To forestall resentment and/or insanity, it's very important to give yourself permission to go to bat for those things that are essential to you.

Short-step # 6 — Step Out of the Way and Out of the Middle

When others have conflicts, step out of the middle by learning to say "Sorry, this isn't my problem. That's between you and him. Work it out." And then actually *let* them either work stuff out or not. In my family, I finally learned to say, "If there's no blood, I don't want to hear about it!" and a favorite of both Gene's and mine, "Take it outside!"

If you feel burned out and are beginning to view murder as an attractive option, move out of the way by taking a time out. Take care of yourself. Rest, regroup, recharge, and wait until you really feel ready for "time in." Chances are everyone will survive and be okay when you energetically return to the fold. In fact they just might learn how to fend for themselves a little more.

Short-step # 7 — Step Lightly

Humor is a lifesaver and a leavening agent. Introduce humor into almost any situation and the energy loosens and lightens up. Most of us are at least a little bit funny and will become even more so if applauded and appreciated for the sparks of humor we show. Kids love to make us laugh, and humor is a significant way they can contribute to the well-being of the family. My son Brett was a notoriously messy kid, which was difficult for Gene to deal with. But one day when checking Brett's room, Gene saw "WILL CLEAN" written in clothes in the middle of the floor and just had to laugh. An irritating habit had been lightened by laughter.

Another extremely meaningful way to step lightly is to view each family member as a gift in our lives. Sometimes we may feel there are a few "gifts" we'd like to return for a refund, but, nonetheless, the more we can be grateful for the "present" inherent in each person's presence, the more light we will shine on their very being, and our own as well. During difficult times, we might ask, "What gift is life and/or this person offering me right now?" I find it powerful and transformative to add, "I can't see the gift in this right now, but I give thanks anyway." Perceiving everyone, including ourselves, as a gift helps us to savor the joys of stepmothering more fully and survive the sorrows more easily.

Short-step # 8 — Step Over

One of the things we women do beautifully is to step over chasms created by misunderstanding, hurt feelings, and poor communication to help create connections between the people whom we care about and between ourselves and others. Because relationships are our lifeblood, women are tremendously invested in the emotional well-being of the family and thrive in an atmosphere of openness, trust, and compassion. As long as we don't feel used and abused by the process, the ability to mediate between family members and between others and ourselves is an important gift that we can offer. However, if you feel like you've become the designated target or that you're caught in the middle and your services are rejected rather than requested, step out of the mediator role.

These short-steps by no means include all those you will be asked to take in your stepmother journey, but I hope they offer you hints, handholds, and helps for the stages of stepping you encounter along the way.

FACING AND AFFIRMING FEELINGS

Taking our stepmother journey one step at a time also often means taking, facing, and affirming our feelings one feeling at a time. Each stepmom I talked with agreed that dealing with her own feelings was a huge issue in merging families. A few moms felt proud of their ability to quickly understand their feelings and keep themselves on an even keel. Most of us, however, experience a myriad of discombobulating feelings from anger and exhaustion, to being overwhelmed, and confused.

Asked what she felt during the first months of her stepmothering career, Nadine chuckled. She felt as if she'd been thrown into a very deep, cold lake. "Although my friends marveled at how calm I looked and how well I seemed to be managing my new marriage and new kids, inside I was drowning." She continued, "I was overwhelmed with all of the added physical and emotional demands placed on me and didn't know, from one moment to the next, if I could keep my head above water. And then, of course, I was worried about my own kids. Were they drowning too? But, you know, I was too scared to ask them. Because if they were, I didn't think I had enough ballast for all of us."

Whereas Nadine experienced a tidal wave of feelings, Shelby, a stepmother-emeritus, told me that during her stepmother career she was so exhausted from being the primary breadwinner, emotional caretaker, and Jill-of-all-trades that she didn't have the energy to know what she felt. "Numb and tired is how I felt," she said. "Oh, wait! Occasionally, I was aware that I felt frustrated and resentful." Shelby offers a good lesson for us all. If we do too much for too many people and don't work to correct the unfairness, resentment is sure to be the result. Shelby's thirty-five year marriage has survived but only barely. Although, over the years, she has learned to stand up for herself and set realistic limits, there are still lingering wounds that may never be healed.

Of course we all know that, intertwined with the vexations, there are fabulous feelings and experiences that we can happily embrace and enjoy. The feelings causing us sleepless nights and clenched jaws, however, are the ones that need transforming.

All Feelings Are Okay, All Actions Are Not

As both a psychotherapist and a stepmother, I want to reiterate the idea that *all* feelings are okay. No matter how icky or ugly, how hateful or appalling our feelings are, they are nothing to feel guilty or ashamed about.

While all feelings are acceptable, destructively acting them out is not. The ability to feel our feelings—no matter how awesomely outrageous—and to choose to act in a responsible and loving manner is a sign of maturity.

Acting maturely may sometimes mean "getting the hell outta Dodge" if we think we might lose control. Rather than doing something we'll regret, we need to leave the situation and the area until we are calm enough to be reasonable. When hot under the collar, taking a walk, soaking in a hot bath, meditating, or simply removing ourself from the proximity of whomever we're angry with is a wise choice. Allowing our feelings to cool before communicating them leads to the possibility of greater understanding, not greater defensiveness.

Of course, positive feelings are better for our health and peace of mind, but believe me no one escapes the "baddies" at all times and in all situations. It's neither fair nor realistic to expect ourselves to continually feel magnanimous and consistently exude sweetness and light.

Running the Gamut of Emotions

As we leap in our rubber raft and navigate down the sometimes placid and often turbulent river of stepmothering, we will experience a full gamut of emotions. Some will be welcome and others will not. A key struggle for all women—and stepmoms in particular—is allowing ourselves to feel what we *really* feel. Our expectations about our feelings may not match the reality of our experience. When we expect to feel loving and accepting and feel ticked off and judgmental instead, it's hard not to be disappointed and disapprove of ourselves. But internal criticism merely exacerbates the fear that we are not good enough, wise enough, loving enough, patient enough, or whatever enough.

Even though we feel the gamut of emotions, we *are* good enough, wise enough, loving enough, and patient enough. We are all those good things and more—we're also human. As humans, we experience all emotions, and, as women, we need to give ourselves permission to be *real* and deal with the reality of our feelings. Attempting to be who we aren't or to feel what we don't really feel, sabotages our self-esteem and diminishes our ability to have honest and loving relationships with others.

The Best Way Out is Always Through

"The best way out is always through" wrote the poet Robert Frost.[1] I think that is a flawless way to face and affirm our feelings. We move through our feelings best when we:

- Face our true feelings.
- Affirm our feelings through acceptance and sharing.
- Act on and express our feelings constructively.
- Allow our feelings to transform and transmute.
- Learn the lessons our feelings offer.

Let's take a closer look at each of these aspects of moving through our feelings.

Facing our true feelings

Facing the fact that she didn't like a new stepson was one of the hardest things Pam ever had to do. "I thought I would always like all kids," she said sadly. "But I didn't like him. He was mean and nasty. His mom was going to put him in a foster home if we didn't take him, so what were we to do?" Having the courage to tell her husband, Chet, about her feelings gave them the opportunity to be honest with each other and decide what course of action would work best for everyone. Although things were never great with this child, they could have been much more stressful had Pam not been able to face her feelings, accept them, and share them with her husband.

With gentle compassion and without judgment, give yourself permission to become aware of your true and honest feelings. Inner awareness is the beginning of outer change. Repressed or suppressed feelings tend to grow in the deep recesses of our minds, becoming unpredictable and unmanageable. In contrast, recognized feelings are out in the open and, therefore, can be courageously faced and moved through.

Affirming feelings through acceptance and sharing

Feelings are flighty. Sometimes we're comfortable with them and often we're not. Feelings are transitory, ever changing emotional responses to situations, circumstances, internal promptings, and other people. Intense feelings scare us because we wonder if we'll always feel this way. When we understand that feelings are transitory, we can become more comfortable with studying them. When we genuinely and lovingly recognize and accept our feelings and say, "Ah, so there you are. What do you want to tell me?" our feelings become more movable and malleable.

After discovering a true feeling, the next step is to affirm and accept the feeling for ourselves and then share it with a trusted friend or counselor. Honestly revealing our feelings to someone who will not judge or criticize them can help us see them more clearly. Sharing our feelings also changes the isolation and loneliness that often come with harboring "secret" and "unacceptable" feelings.

Tamara felt guilty for being angry with some of her adult children. A friend with whom she shared her guilt and anger responded, "I know! I often feel that way about my adult daughter." As the two friends talked, Tamara's guilt and anger diminished and she became aware of some changes she would like to make in her own behavior toward her kids. However, to honor our vulnerability and keep ourselves safe, we need to carefully choose the people with whom we share ourselves. Often stepparenting groups are the perfect place in which to open up.

Acting on and expressing feelings constructively

I can't stress enough how important it is to *constructively* express and act on our feelings. In my therapy practice, I have seen many relationships destroyed because people who supposedly loved each other could not learn to express their difficult feelings effectively. It's often necessary to siphon off intense emotional energy before trying to have a discussion with those who need to know what we're feeling. (Stunning someone with the full force of our powerful feelings naturally makes them withdraw or respond defensively.) Such energy can be effectively tempered in many ways: aerobic exercise, screaming in a safe place, beating pillows, crying, or talking to a friend or therapist, to name a few. Although it's important to express ourselves and our feelings, it is equally important that we never express or act at the expense of another person or in ways that are destructive to relationships that we value.

Allowing your feelings to transform and transmute

Some feelings are just too juicy to let go of, little burrs under our saddles that hurt so good, a few prize injustices that make our martyrdom so attractive. I say that facetiously, but there can be real danger in holding onto a pet peeve or grievance. We risk learning to love the identity such feelings provide for us, whether it's victim, overworked Cinderella, martyr, resentful rebel, or depressed woman. None of these identities will help us manage and enjoy our lives, to say nothing of our stepfamilies.

Tired of feeling resentful toward her husband and his children for what she perceived as their lack of appreciation, Clarice sought help from her minister. Together they decided that each time she noticed resentment festering Clarice would send a "love dart" of good wishes or blessings toward the object of her consternation. After several weeks of love-dart-sending, Clarice reported, "My resentment really mellowed and I was simply able to tell the kids and my husband how I would like to be appreciated."

If you are holding onto a favorite negative feeling, please bring it into the light of understanding and acceptance so that it can be transformed and transmuted into the perfect energy for your life. If letting go seems impossible, talk to someone who can help you work through the issue and put it to rest.

Learning the lessons our feelings offer

Our feelings don't just spring from anywhere. If we pay attention to them, we'll see that our feelings call attention to unresolved issues within us, wounds that still need tending, and circumstances in our lives that require change. When we deny or suppress our feelings, they can't teach us the lessons we need to know.

I, for example, try to avoid anger as much as possible. Consequently, in order to learn anger's lessons, I need to be repeatedly banged on the head. Many Christmases ago my stepdaughter Paige wielded a hammer heavy enough to get my attention. I had carefully shopped for presents that I hoped she'd like. But when she unwrapped a sweater with a small red stripe on it and said, "I hate red," I *saw* red. But I also finally learned the lesson of that anger. I'd tried too hard and taken too much for too many years. I was done. That afternoon I informed Gene that from now on anything having to do with Paige would be done by him. I backed off entirely, leaving her to hate me in peace, which to tell the truth, was a relief to us both. Thankfully, we were eventually able to turn toward each other with affection, but that took many years.

BREAKING THE WORRY HABIT

Now let's take a closer look at one "feeling" that often keeps stepmothering from being enjoyable and manage-able—worry. I put feeling in quotation marks, because worry is really more of a habit than a feeling, though unidentified feelings often underlie our worrying. Where does our worry come from, and how can we break the worry habit?

In her book *The Worrywart's Companion,* Dr. Beverly Potter states, "The job of worry is to anticipate danger before it arises and to identify possible perils, to come up with ways to lessen the risks, and to rehearse what you plan to do. Worrywarts get stuck in identifying danger."[2] Dr. Potter helps us see that, more often than not, worry is unnecessary.

Worry is a habit that shatters our peace of mind and needlessly drains our energy, a form of mind masturbation without the benefits. Engrossed in worry, our attention is riveted on the unchangeable past or struggling with an imagined future. Worrying casts us out of the here and now and sends us skittering into the often catastrophic "What if's" and "Oh, my gods" of the unknowable yet-to-come. Since most habits are learned, it's important for us to ask where we learned to worry.

A new stepmom, Rhonda found herself worrying about every possible scenario that her stepfamily might go through. She worried that things might never change, or if they did change, they might get worse. "I'm anxious all the time. What if the kids turn out to be really rebellious teenagers? What if their mother decides they should live with us?" she asked, obviously in pain. I suggested we table those questions and look, instead, at who taught her to worry. "Well, Mother, of course." she answered. From her mother, Rhonda absorbed powerful beliefs: Life is difficult; there is never enough to go around; no one can be trusted; God is a punishing and vengeful father; and she, Rhonda, was unlovable. Weaned on fear, was it any wonder that Rhonda worried? Worry is fear made visible and/or audible.

As we talked, Rhonda saw how her worrying was born from her mother's belief system, not her own. When I asked, "Do you really believe that?" she could honestly answer "no" to most of the scary assumptions she inherited. Bolstered by those insights, Rhonda decided to befriend herself by breaking the worry habit.

As with any chronic worrier, Rhonda needs to intervene quickly when her worry habit begins to assert itself. She's learned to do so by, first, pulling her mind and attention back into the present moment where her worry is not a reality. She then assures herself that she can handle what is actually taking place right now. If she can't handle the present situation constructively or with ease, she takes time out and goes for a walk, meditates, breathes deeply, or delves into her own work. Next, Rhonda asks herself what fears and beliefs caused her worry. If they belong to her mom, she blesses her mother and evicts her from her mind. If the fear is her own, she explores it. Rhonda's final intervention is a wonderful remedy for fear and chronic worry. She affirms her underlying faith that the Universe is friendly, that the Universal Mystery is *for* her rather than against her, and that she is, indeed, lovable.

Rhonda's commitment to breaking her worry habit is working. Her stepchildren have not come to live with them full-time and "I don't even think about when they'll be teenagers anymore," she informed me. Good for her.

There is one kind of worry, however, that should be heeded. If we are worrying about something we've done or said in the past, our spirits may be encouraging us to make amends. Although we can't change history, we can apologize and clear the air. And once we do so, that worry can be laid to rest.

Because we are the authors of our own thoughts, we can break the worry habit. We can consciously *choose* not to drift into the future or fall back into the past. As a Chinese proverb states, "That the birds of worry and care fly above your head, this you cannot change ... but that they build nests in your hair, this you can prevent."[3]

CHOOSING THE HIGH ROAD

While it is essential that we honor and acknowledge our real feelings each step of the way, it's also possible for us to adjust our feelings by elevating our attitude. Adopting a positive attitude allows us to choose the high road of optimism and affection.

Life's "high road" is constructed from the building blocks of a positive attitude, continual gratitude, appreciation for the wonder of life itself, enthusiasm and amusement for and about almost anything, looking on the bright side, a deep love and acceptance of ourselves and others, and an abiding intention to understand and learn from our experiences. By contrast, the "low road" is paved with negativity, victimization, and an attitude of blame and recrimination.

We build the "roads" through our feelings with our thoughts and attitudes. While we don't have total control over many other things, we are the sole creator of our thoughts—the only thinker in our lives. *We* are in charge of our attitudes. Since feelings are a direct result of attitudes and thoughts, the ability to choose what is on our minds is one of our most precious and useful attributes. Given time and perhaps some guidance, we can learn to choose "Isn't this interesting?" instead of "Isn't it awful?" We can decide to be amused more often than appalled. A positive attitude brings peace of mind whereas a negative attitude fosters chaos and confusion.

While not easy, changing our minds is as simple as changing the channel on the television. Since thought patterns and attitudes can become deeply ingrained within us, changing our minds requires a deep commitment on our part to pay attention to our thoughts and, without judgment, switch a negative thought such as, "I hate this. These kids are messy monsters who are ruining my life," to a more positive and accepting one, "Kids will be kids, so what do I need to do right now to feel better?" The first statement will probably keep us stuck in negative feelings while the second one not only gives us perspective but also encourages us to take care of ourselves.

At each bend, twist, and turn of the stepmothering journey, we are given new opportunities to choose either the high road or the low road. Taking the high road means that we pay close attention to the positive elements of our lives, consistently look for what we can learn about ourselves and others during difficult times, and gently and lovingly take care of ourselves. Doing these things not only makes us stronger and happier but also insures that we will be more loving and fun to live with.

I know as well as anyone that sometimes we're just too darned tired and discouraged to do anything but make it through the next ten minutes. But even those few minutes are filled with choices. We can take a much needed time out, rest, meditate, pray, call a friend, or collapse semicomatose under an afghan with a cup of tea. I see all those choices as the taking the high road. In contrast, the low road might include yelling at the kids, berating our husbands, drinking or eating too much, driving too fast, or castigating ourselves about real and imagined failures.

Gratitude is one of the most beneficial high road attitudes we can develop. With gratitude as our perspective, it's easier to remain open to the adventures stepmothering offers. Gratitude gives us the strength to leap more nimbly over the pits of emotional quicksand. It also helps us develop a positive, accepting, and loving attitude toward ourselves, which often insures that we will be able to embrace the same attitude toward others, our stepchildren included.

Although it's probably not a lesson learned at your mother's knee, it is, nonetheless, of primary importance that you learn how to take excellent care of yourself and value your own well-being. The well-being and success of your entire combined family is enhanced when you take kind and loving care of yourself. And this becomes a lesson your children and stepchildren can learn from you—one step at a time.

PART THREE

Taking Care Of Yourself

Love yourself first and everything else falls into line. You really have to love yourself to get anything done in this world.

—LUCILLE BALL

Judging from my own experience and other stepmoms I've spoken with, women who are actively stepmothering today are a great deal more aware of the need to take care of themselves than women were ten or twenty years ago. While I'm tickled that women are more aware of the importance of self-care, I also realize that it's still difficult for most of us to actually *do* it. We're talkin' a better talk but not walkin' a much better walk.

Maybe understanding that one of the most beneficial results of self-care is an increased ability to love others will help us care for ourselves more gently and completely. Self-love is not selfishness or self-centeredness. Quite the contrary. Accepting, approving of, and appreciating ourselves seems to generate a reservoir of goodwill and loving kindness that naturally spills over to benefit our family members, friends, and colleagues.

Actually, the reservoir metaphor is an apt one for stepmothering. In few other relationships are so many asked to do so much for so little recognition or reward. We may do the mothering but never be thought of as a mother. We may do all the right things but receive very little credit. We may also care a great deal and yet have very few rights. Not that we accept the role merely for the recognition, credit, and reward. No, we accept it because we love the children's father. Nonetheless, we need to realize that all of us want and need acknowledgement, recognition, and appreciation to replenish our reservoirs. Because stepmoms are expected to pour forth regularly but refills are often infrequent, it's crucial that we learn how to fill our own reservoirs. That way we can happily share our abundance with others and not be depleted in the process.

What fills you? What pumps up your energy level and makes your heart sing? Or, equally important, what calms, soothes, rests, and rejuvenates you? Stepmoms cite their work, friends, other family members, and therapy and/or support groups as the primary ways they take care of and replenish themselves. High on the list of helpful skills is becoming less sensitive to criticism and slights by remembering "This isn't about me!" One woman found watching Don Johnson in *Nash Bridges* soothing and another stated that Excedrin became her best friend. Whatever works...

As the stepmom to a nine-year-old girl, Penny offered this intelligent advice, "Take care of yourself. Do not let yourself get isolated. I did, and it nearly did me in. Get the bigger picture by checking in with other stepparents. If you don't, it's easy to make mountains out of molehills. Above all, don't take it all so seriously!" I can't think of better advice as we try to take care of ourselves.

Being A True Friend To Yourself

Where am I when I need me most?
—MUGS HOLIFIELD

A faithful friend sees the good, true, and beautiful within us and reflects our light back to us when we perceive only darkness. A dear and trusted friend encourages us to be our best self while also helping us face the worst both within and around us. Devoted friends hold us when we weep and dance with us in joy. Friends build us up and accentuate our highest qualities. Friends delight in us. For women, such friendships are not luxuries but absolute necessities; they anchor us in reality, soar with us in silliness and celebration, support us as needed, and assist us in becoming the people we were created to be.

The big question is, Are you such a friend to yourself? To get a sense of how true a friend you are to yourself, please see how many of these questions you can answer affirmatively:

- Are you encouraging rather than critical?
- Do you matter-of-factly accept your mistakes as opportunities to learn valuable lessons, master them, and then move on with a little pat on your own back?
- Are you gentle and kind to yourself?

- Do you realize when you're worn out and allow yourself to rest and replenish?
- Do you make time to express your unique creativity?
- Do you honor who and what you are?
- Can you make realistic and gentle to-do lists and then follow them?
- Do you know what you want and need from others and allow yourself to ask for it?
- Can you stand up for yourself when necessary?
- Do you accept only acceptable behavior toward yourself?
- Will you seek help from either professionals or family and friends when you need it?
- Do you surround yourself with like-minded people?
- Do you usually act in a manner that makes you proud of yourself?

In other words, can you count on yourself to be there when you need you most? Befriending ourselves is probably the most important task we can undertake. Self-love and acceptance fill our reservoirs, while nothing drains and dries them faster than being either a lackadaisical, occasional friend or our own worst enemy.

SETTING PRIORITIES FOR OURSELVES

Contrary to what we've traditionally been taught, we need to put ourselves at the head of our priority list, to take care of ourselves and our soul's growth in order to better love and care for others. We're told to put our own oxygen mask on first and our child's second in case of an airplane emergency, because if we don't care for ourselves, we can't really help anyone else. Of course, sometimes giving everything to others *will* be your first priority. With little babies and during illness, death, trauma, injury, or emotional distress, we naturally prioritize accordingly. Even then, after continually giving, any caregiver—from an intensive care nurse to a hospice professional—must rest and replenish or risk becoming ill or overly exhausted herself. Rare are the instances in which sacrifice is both desirable and rewarding. In regular day to day life, persistent sacrifice is usually detrimental to the well-being of everyone involved.

As a psychotherapist, mom, and stepmom who gathered wisdom from other stepmothers, I've developed the following prioritized list for caregiving:

Caregiving in ordinary day-to-day life
1. Self: Fill your own reservoir.
2. Marriage: Nurture and strengthen your relationship with your husband. The two of you will be together when the children are grown.
3. Your own children: Your responsibility to your children is primary.
4. Your stepchildren: These children have parents. When they are in your home, rely heavily on your

husband to care for them. If he is unavailable, care for them as you do your own children.

Caregiving under extraordinary circumstances
1. Whoever is acutely in need.
2. Self.
3. Whoever is left.

During his senior year in high school my son Brett sustained a knee injury that required a series of serious surgeries and squashed his dream of becoming a professional athlete. Two weeks later his older brother, Mike, developed Bell's Palsy. Reputable doctors warned Mike that the right side of his face might never be mobile again, which smashed to smithereens his dreams of an acting career. Before these misfortunes, both boys had the talent and background to bring their dreams to fruition. As their mother, my heart was broken.

As a mother lion, I was damned sure my cubs would not become prisoners of any doctor's dire predictions. With assertiveness I didn't know I possessed, I found the best knee surgeon around for Brett and sought out cutting-edge alternative therapy for Mike. I'm sure, if purgatory exists, it can't be any harder than those next months. Under those extraordinary circumstances, my priorities were clear: Mike and Brett, and somewhere way down the line, me. I had nothing left for anyone or anything else.

When or if your caregiving coffers give out, you may be surprised at how well everyone can get along without your ministering. Gene and the girls managed to get along just fine while I concentrated on the boys' needs. And another time, I was flat-on-my-back sick for ten days and was humbled and chagrined at how smoothly Gene and the kids made out after the first day or two. Learning I wasn't indispensable proved to be a valuable lesson for us all.

Setting priorities that keep ourselves lovingly in mind not only makes sure that we are strong and balanced but also gives a beautiful message to the other members of our families: It is okay to value yourself and keep yourself well, happy, and creatively active. Being around a mother who befriends herself and takes as much care of herself as she does of others provides a powerful model for both children and husbands.

HONORING YOUR IDENTITY AND AUTHENTICITY

You had a pre-stepmother self. Is she still your friend? Is she still alive and well and expressing herself freely, or has she become a mere shadow of her former self? Because it was many years ago, I'm surprised now by my reaction to these questions. Tears swim in my eyes, tears for my young stepmother self who put on a good front but felt so lost and lousy much of the time.

I know that part of my fear and insecurity during those early years sprang from unhealed wounds sustained when my first husband left me for my best friend. Following that swift kick in the psyche, countless tears, much therapy, and graduate school all contributed to my learning—for the first time in my adult years—who I really was and discovering I liked that someone. To my dismay, self-doubt, low self-esteem, insecurity, and fear began to take root in my heart again as soon as I found a man whom I couldn't bear the thought of losing.

For many of us, losing ourselves in relationships is an age-old dilemma: Can I love you without losing me? The answer is, "Yes, but ..." Yes, but our dedication to ourselves must be strong and unwavering. With so many other people, predicaments, and priorities that need our time and attention, it can be hard to hold on to our own identity and honor our unique authenticity.

After writing these paragraphs, awash in a resurgence of old feelings, I needed to leave my computer and do a small prayer/meditation practice. I put my hands over my heart and sent love and acceptance to my former self, offering her solace and support in face of the emotions that had resurfaced. My reaction reminds me that it's so important to realize that we don't achieve friendship with self and then announce, "Okay, that's done!" and live happily ever after. More than any other relationship, our friendship with our selves is a life-long and daily commitment to caring, growth, and discovery.

Finding and Sustaining the Real You

But what if we don't have a clue who we really are? If we've spent our entire life pleasing others and doing what we thought was expected of us, there's a good chance that we're not fully in touch with who we are and who we are meant to become. If that's the case with you, falling in love and marrying a man with children will give you ample opportunity to remain in the dark about your authentic self—unless you make a conscious effort to bring yourself to light.

Grace was only twenty and, by her own admission, very naive when she married her thirty-five-year-old employer and began mothering his teenage sons part-time. She was thirty-five, with two biological children, when I talked with her. Very emotionally, she shared that only in the last three years had she realized that she'd been identifying herself only in terms of her roles: wife, mother, and stepmother. "I was depressed and unhappy and didn't know why," she said. "It was my husband who suggested I go to therapy, and reluctantly I agreed." Wryly, she added, "I think he's quite sorry now, because I'm not sure I can stay married and keep the me I've finally found. It's hard on us all. But we're all in counseling, and I think we'll make it." With a sweet smile, she continued, "You know, even with all of the upset and turmoil we're in, I feel more alive than I ever have. I'm beginning to really like and accept this Grace I never knew."

I'm not surprised that things are difficult for Grace and her family right now. Pain and difficulty are natural to birth and, after giving birth to two children and caring for two more, Grace is now giving birth to her authentic self. As a part of her metamorphosis, Grace has gone to college and is learning to fill her reservoir from the wells of her own creativity and passion.

Creativity and Passion

One of the best ways to befriend yourself and realize who you truly are is discovering where your passions lie and how your creativity wants to express itself in the world. At the very center of our being are creative sparks that link us inexorably to our Source, the Creator/Creatrix. Creativity is our kinship to God. When we follow our passions and create in ways that make our hearts sing, we express our authentic selves. In fact, the blessing of freeing our creative spirit is that it reconnects us to the power that each of us has at birth. Our birthright is to be a creative woman.

"Squeezing in time for sewing and baking," seventy-five year old Angie told me, "was the way I took care of myself and remembered who I was." Unfortunately, Angie's stepfamily was very adversarial early on. Her husband and his daughter would "gang up on me," she sighed. But, although life was often painful, Angie was able to follow a friend's advice: "You must not allow other people's limited perceptions of you to define you."

Angie expressed her authentic self through her career and squeezing in time for her beloved sewing and baking. Now, she enthused, "It was all worth it, every iota of pain and work!" Had she not befriended herself and retained her identity during the hard times by doing what she loved, Angie probably would not have been able to answer so positively.

When was the last time you lost track of time while doing something you love? Time does seem to fly when we're fully engaged in a creative endeavor that touches our souls. Such interests can range from traveling or studying certain topics to painting or interior decorating. It doesn't matter what form your creativity takes. For me, it's playing with words. For Angie, it was baking and sewing, while some women's gardens are outer expressions of their own inner beauty. One such woman is Clawdia.

In speaking about her now-defunct stepfamily, Clawdia (a pseudonym she requested "because I felt like my claws were out all the time") said, "Without my garden, I might have gone crazy." Among her roses, Clawdia was in touch with who she really was. And it was surrounded by the beauty of her garden that Clawdia wept the question, "Should I leave this marriage?" Looking up to see a double rainbow in an otherwise clear sky seemed like an affirmation that, yes, for both her own and her daughter's sake, she needed to leave.

As with Clawdia's garden, the flowering of your creativity may not only make your own soul sigh with happiness but also create a beautiful place or thing that brings solace and inspiration to others. Working at what we love and pursuing those activities and interests that fire our passion and creativity can be as much a gift to others as to ourselves, and that gift is the gift of wholeness.

CULTIVATING WHOLENESS

"Women's work is always toward wholeness." muses Mrs. Stevens in May Sarton's novel, *Mrs. Stevens Hears the Mermaids Singing*.[1] Moving toward wholeness is both the unique beauty of a woman's character and the root of her deepest frustration. By our very nature, we are drawn to the ideal of wholeness for ourselves and for the entire human family. At the core of our being, we carry a soul-memory of wholeness, which is embodied by our deep and holy hunger for love. We long for heart-centered, meaningful connections with ourselves, others, and God, whom I like to call The Beloved. One of the ways we take care of ourselves is by moving toward this heart-centeredness, this wholeness.

Although we yearn for wholeness, as a general rule, our culture often discourages our yearning through ignorance, lack of attention, and unfair stereotypes, such as those surrounding stepmothering. In Western society, feminine contributions, like mothering and nurturing, are often invisible and unpaid. And, of course, pay is the equivalent of value in our culture. The devaluation of feminine qualities cheats our families, stepfamilies, and ourselves out of the softer and more nourishing attributes inherent to wholeness. As a result, women often question themselves, their most sacred desires, and the gifts they have to give.

When we are neither aware of our inner selves nor encouraged to move toward wholeness, we are severed from the root of who we are and can't discover who we are capable of becoming. I believe it is this severing from the soul that is the unconscious cause of many women's frustration, depression, and anger.

It's easy to be anesthetized by both the real and self-created demands from society, career, and family, and to lose sight of who we authentically are—eternal spiritual beings taking human form for our soul's growth. As women first and stepmoms second, it's essential to befriend and take care of ourselves by shaking free of any numbness that's settling on our souls and recognize our spiritual yearning for wholeness. Becoming more conscious of our real selves opens a window to soul and invites more meaning, health, happiness, and love into all of our relationships.

Knowing that wholeness is our heart's desire and that love is the path to wholeness allows us to more readily say "yes" to the soul work inherent in the roles of wife and stepmother and to view our experiences from a different, perhaps higher, perspective. Adopting a spiritual viewpoint doesn't guarantee that life will be easier, but it does mean we are more likely to find meaning and growth within our experiences, and, consequently, accept them more graciously.

Illuminating the Shadow

To become truly whole, we need to embrace all aspects of ourselves, light and shadow alike. Most of us can easily accept the agreeable and virtuous facets of ourselves. It is the darker and more disturbing aspects of our being that we want to lock away in a cellar. We've absorbed our society's message: light is okay, but shadow is not.

According to noted Swiss psychiatrist, Carl Jung, the shadow parts of ourselves are undeveloped or denied aspects of our being that need to be acknowledged. If we were brought up to be "nice" girls, for example, we were also taught to be ashamed of our shadow—our rage, assertiveness, ambition, sexuality, even our creativity. Denying, repressing, and disowning these aspects gnaws at our well-being and sense of wholeness. When denied, our shadow gains strength and becomes almost diabolical in its ability to cause us, and others, pain.

Yet our shadows are not boogie-women, as we may have been led to believe; rather they are orphaned aspects of ourselves crying out for reunion. Our shadow contains vast gifts, talents, and potential as well as wounded and deformed personality parts. Embracing our shadowy aspects and learning to express them constructively transforms their energy and allows them to merge with the rest of our self and create wholeness. Without our shadow, we are only half our selves.

If you are not certain what your shadow aspects are, your stepchildren can probably help you identify them. Most stepchildren are highly creative shadow-spotters and can shine a light into the basement of your being with piercing acuity. Given that talent, they can be among our greatest teachers.

"Stepmothering introduced me to parts of myself that I didn't know existed and never wanted to become acquainted with," said Linda, stepmother to a boy and girl. "I had never been around kids much and these two pushed buttons I didn't even know I had." She continued, "I didn't even recognize the uptight, over-controlling bitch I became. I hated the kid's messiness. I hated the fact that they didn't appreciate the things I did for them. I hated *them!* And then, of course, I hated me for hating them."

Luckily, Linda and her husband found a stepparenting group where Linda learned that she wasn't alone in her reactions, that the shadow roamed in many other stepmoms as well. The group helped Linda accept her feelings and reassured her husband, Al, that the wonderful woman he loved had not turned forever into a "Mrs. Hyde." With the group's help, Linda uncovered ways to take care of herself in her new and very different lifestyle. "I came to realize and accept that I'm a person who needs a lot of quiet, space, and time alone. At first, I didn't allow myself those when the kids were with us, but now I do and we all benefit. Al gets quality time with his kids and a wife who is no longer a monster." She added, with a laugh, "I've earned the right to be called by my first name now instead of PMS, which stood for Pretty Mean Stepmother."

Linda is not unique. Inexperienced, childless stepmothers are often shocked by the shadow aspects of themselves that surge forward in the presence of children. Many are also pleased and gratified by the depth of love and connection they eventually feel for these same kids.

There are many ways to cultivate wholeness and befriend our shadow by bringing it into the light of our love. A stepparenting group can be very helpful, as it was for Linda and Al. For me, writing in my journal proved a lifesaver. During difficult times, I could pour all of my feelings onto its pages, safely and constructively releasing pent up, powerful emotions. Journaling can be an emotional garbage dump as well as a refuge, a safe place in which our shadow sides can scream or sob.

At times I journaled toward sanity and stability. Other times, I visualized the aspects of myself that were having difficulty and dialogued with them to find out what they wanted and needed from me, what they feared, how they felt abandoned by me, and what positive quality they might bring to my life. For instance, when I felt jealous because Gene seemed to be choosing his daughters over me, I asked to be shown the person within me who was experiencing the painful feelings. More often than not, I "saw" my own inner little girl who had sometimes felt abandoned by her daddy and was now afraid that Gene didn't love her and that she might be abandoned by him.

Although it was often a painful process, I'm so thankful for the gift of having stepdaughters. The girls were my greatest mirrors into the shadows of my past. Their femaleness helped me become aware of and heal wounds I still carried from childhood. The way Gene related to and loved Lynnie and Paige forced me to excavate old disappointments, make peace with them, and become incredibly grateful for the love and security that I did have in my growing-up years.

In our quest for wholeness, we need to accept and transform our ever-present shadow, that, like the dark side of the moon, is the hidden half of our beings. It is up to us to liberate and illuminate her. Our stepfamily situations give us many opportunities to become aware of our shadow sides, but you, and only you, know the avenues of healing and exploration most beneficial for you. Become quiet and ask the wisdom of your heart to lead you as you seek to illuminate your unique shadow selves. If you have difficulty discovering which way to go, please have the courage to ask for help.

Hoops of Steel

Women are relational beings. We thrive when encircled by supportive family and friends. For that very reason, we could take Polonius's advice to Laertes, "Those friends thou hast, and their adoption tried, grapple them unto thy soul with hoops of steel."[2] Separated from the protective and encouraging presence of those she loves, it is easy for a woman to feel isolated and lonely.

The stepmothers I talked to who had the hardest time adjusting to their new lives and children were those who left familiar surroundings in order to be with the man of their dreams. Those who stayed in their own homes and/or towns and maintained regular contact with old and trusted friends made the transition more smoothly. I was in the first group.

Mike, Brett, and I moved to Hawaii to be with Gene, Paige, and Lynnie. Sounds romantic, doesn't it? And it was. But it was also traumatic. All of the adjustments to a new locale were intensified by the boys' grief over being separated from their father and my loneliness for dear friends with whom I could honestly discuss the good stuff and the hard stuff that inevitably comes with new relationships.

From my own experience of lacking support during the onset of our stepfamily, I know that we women need to "grapple" old and dear friends to our souls "with hoops of steel" as we begin our stepping. Of course, many of Gene's friends welcomed me with open arms, and I appreciated them immensely, but they were not yet *my* friends and I didn't feel comfortable opening my heart and soul to them until we were better acquainted.

Social and emotional isolation makes adjustment to stepfamily life incredibly difficult. Many stepmoms underscored the importance of breaking out of isolation and finding friendship and support for themselves and, at times, the whole family. In fact, these moms believe they might not make it without being in therapy, having a circle of friends with whom they can share honestly, or attending stepmother or stepparenting groups. "If I wasn't in a stepmom's group," said Jenny, "I would go crazy. Just seeing their heads nods as I cry or complain makes me feel less alone and more able to cope. I learn a lot from them, and they continually give me hope."

With very few exceptions, stepmothers told me their women friends were a major support system at all times but especially as they weathered the first few years of creating a cohesive, complementary family unit. Although understanding and supportive husbands are incredibly important to a stepmother's peace of mind and well-being, individual women friends or circles of friends are invaluable companions and counselors.

While the wise adage says it takes a village to raise a child, it also takes a village to help build and sustain a stepfamily—an empathetic circle of friends and acquaintances who understand, love, and guide us. As gentle and true friends to ourselves, we must find supportive circles from which we can gather the encouragement and insight we need in order to create the wholeness for which we yearn.

The relationship that most needs our tender love, acceptance, and understanding is our friendship with ourselves. Our security and our ability to love and be of service to others all flow from it. In fact, there is no real or lasting security except that which we build inside ourselves. Building a gentle and true friendship within the boundaries of our own being insures that real security is always with us. From that strength, we can weave the future with today's threads of acceptance, growth, and authenticity. With insight and help, we can be today what we will be proud of tomorrow.

Setting (and Sticking To) Limits and Boundaries

Unless someone truly has the power to say no, they never truly have the power to say yes.

—DAN MILLMAN

Deciding early on what guidelines operate in your home and then gently but firmly upholding them, can save a lot of grief further along the stepmothering road. Easily said, often not easily done as Erika, who is raising her two children full-time and her two stepchildren half-time, found. With a tired sigh, she told me how hard it was for her to grasp the idea of setting limits and boundaries and expecting them to be honored.

"It's bad enough around the house when just my kids are there, but when Phil's children come, it's bedlam! The noise and mess drives me crazy," she said. "So what are your limits and boundaries about the noise and mess?" I asked. Erika looked at me quizzically and said, "Huh? What do you mean?" "How much are you willing to put up with?" I asked. "Kids are naturally pretty noisy and messy, but how much of that can you accept without getting overly uptight and ticked off?" "Well, I mean, you know ... Gosh, I'd never thought of it that way," Erika confessed.

WHERE ARE THE BOUNDARIES?

Like Erika, we may have forgotten that we have both the right and responsibility to set parameters. As kids, we probably accepted our parents' limits and boundaries and knew that we darn well better honor them. But for some strange reason that doesn't always translate into our own mothering and stepmothering. We may realize it's good to set limits and boundaries but, like long-term stepmom Cheryl said, "I knew what to do but didn't have the guts to do it."

It's usually much easier to set limits for our own kids than it is for our stepchildren. Not only have we set limits for them since they were tiny, but we're also familiar with their idiosyncrasies and sure of their love. We *know* our own children, while we must grow to know our stepkids.

Although kids often do everything in their power to resist our authority, they're actually more secure when they know the ground rules. Knowing what is expected of them and what they can expect from you allows everyone to relax a little. Eileen's four children were not allowed to eat sugar or junk food, but her stepson had been "raised on Poptarts and hot dogs," she said. "At first, when he came for the weekends, he sneaked candy in and shared it with my kids. For a while I couldn't understand why everyone was so hyper when Chad was there."

When his smuggling was discovered, Eileen and her husband, Mike, sat down with Chad and told him that the house rules forbade sugar and he was not to bring any with him. Instead of complying, Chad became more inventive about smuggling in his stash. Luckily, Mike honored Eileen's sugar ban for her children and, eventually, they reached a compromise. Mike searched Chad and his luggage when picking him up for visits, confiscated all contraband, and doled out one treat a day to Chad.

As you might suspect, this limit didn't endear Eileen to Chad, but he did grow to respect her wishes. She said, "It seemed like a small thing, but if I hadn't said no to him, I would have compromised my value system and had a much more difficult time accepting him into our home and coming to love him." Being able to say no to Chad made it easier for Eileen to say yes to him in other very important ways. The support of his extended family finally became far sweeter to Chad than sugar had ever been.

In a family, the bottom line is finding ways of being together that foster more love and acceptance for everyone. Optimally, limits and boundaries help us all become more comfortable and therefore better able to love more freely.

What Is Off-Limits?

As I talked with stepmothers, I heard many variations on the theme, "Where did all the quiet, order, and privacy go?" Each stepmom, no matter what her circumstances, admitted that the chaos factor had multiplied exponentially with additional relationships in her life. "Not that I'm complaining, you understand," said Kate. "I wanted him, I wanted them, I wanted all of this, but my head never stops spinning. Adding a man and two more kids to my own two feels like I've added a thousand in terms of noise and work." She added with a perplexed shake of her head, "I love it. It's fun, but they're *everywhere*. And I can never find anything anymore!" I had to laugh because my own long-term lament with the kids was, "Okay, you guys, where's my hair brush?"

Part of setting limits and boundaries is to know when and where to hang an "off-limits" sign. Of course, hanging up the sign doesn't mean anyone will pay attention to it. Eventually, the brush became a running a joke as I found short red hairs or long brown ones amid my own blond strands. However, our bedroom, when the door was closed, and my home office were different stories. There, "off-limits" meant business.

Of course, off-limits needs to be a two-way street. When we expect to have our own space and property respected, we need to act in kind. If we disregard others' off-limits signs, they are likely to return the disfavor.

Everyone requires privacy and a certain amount of literal and emotional space (and teenagers usually demand massive amounts of emotional room).

Give yourself permission to say, "This time or space is sacred to me. It is inviolate—only mine—you are not invited to share it, use it, or come into it." Stating and enforcing such boundaries not only bolsters our self-respect but also helps kids learn respect for others' space, rights, and property.

Stepping Away From Power Struggles

In setting limits and boundaries, it's important that we choose our battles wisely and learn to distinguish between a fair and reasonable rule and a power struggle. Limits and boundaries insure the safety and sanity of all concerned, whereas power struggles orbit around the need to be in control and do just the opposite. You can recognize power struggles by the frustration, tight jaws, and sense of righteousness or impotence that often accompanies them. Statements such as, "Because I said so ...," "Because I'm your mother ...," "It's my house, you'll do as I say ...," or "Because I make the money ..." often connote power struggles.

Food and eating are frequently areas in which power struggles occur between adults and children. The plaintive bleats "Do I have to eat *that*?" or "What's in this?" signal a power struggle is afoot. More direct and less socialized, little kids will simply refuse to eat or throw food on the floor. Between one and two years old my son Mike refused to eat anything but dry cereal. I was aghast and felt like a failure until our pediatrician said, "It's natural. Don't worry, if he's hungry he'll eat." Feelings of frustration, impotence, and confusion often accompany power struggles and, if you're locked in a power struggle with a child of almost any age, I'll bet on the kid.

When setting limits and boundaries, ask yourself if this is a fair and reasonable rule that will benefit everyone in the long run, or is it a power struggle? Here's an example from our family. Our kids all had a curfew. During high school, it was 10:00 p.m. on week nights, but they could stay out until 1:00 a.m. on Friday and Saturday. In the summer, we stretched the curfew to 11:00 p.m. on week nights. We heard every complaint you can imagine from, "You don't trust me" to the old faithful, "But so-and-so doesn't have a curfew!"

Finally, when we explained that the curfew was as much for us as it was for them, they understood we weren't being mean. Neither of us could sleep until all our chickadees were home. And, though our sleeplessness wasn't their fault or responsibility, living with parents who were sleep-deprived would definitely not be good for anyone. If we had been locked in a power struggle, we would have demanded the kids be home at 11:30 p.m. on weekends because *we* would have preferred going to sleep then.

If you notice that you're prone to engaging in power struggles, give yourself a break and practice giving up one power struggle a week, as a client of mine did. With an impish smile, Lela said, "Letting go of power struggles is more fun than I thought it would be. Not only is my TMJ better, but every time one of the kids tries to hook me and I let it pass, it throws 'em for a loop."

Finally, don't take it too personally when the kids either push the prescribed limits or enter into power struggles with you. That's in their job description. Often the struggle isn't about you at all. Ah, how I wish I had integrated that truth into my heart and soul while actively stepmuddling!

KEEPING DAD IN THE LOOP

Stepfamilies are healthier and stepmothers happier and more loving when their husbands actively take part in all facets of family life. When Dad is willing and able to have close and intimate relationships with his wife and the children and backs Mom up in all reasonable ways, marriages are more apt to flourish and, as a result, the kids will feel more secure.

Thankfully, there are husbands, fathers, and stepfathers eager to be a major part of everyone's life and provide emotional support as well. Women whose husbands were enthusiastic about being an integral member of the family and were also able to communicate openly and honestly, raved about how wonderful their men were. Their parenting and stepparenting roles were eased by their husband's friendship and support. Many of these men had made a special effort to learn the art of relationship by seeking out training in communication skills and the ability to relate to various age groups. Their caring commitment is a boon to each family.

With a fond chuckle, Alice said that her husband, Tim, had first been his five stepchildren's schoolteacher, knew them all well, and "thought it would be fun" to inherit all these kids. In fact, Tim and Alice thought parenting was so much fun that they added an "ours" child to his one and her five.

Another great example is Patrick, a nurse, and Sandy, an accountant, who look forward to their couple's therapy sessions where they can safely share all of the turmoil and trauma caused by his four children and their mother. "Patrick's stabilizing influence on my own two kids and his willingness to go to therapy has made all the difference in our relationship," said Sandy. Patrick's sweet Irish grin flashed as he looked at her fondly. It was obvious that, even though they have some difficult challenges, they are committed partners.

On the other hand, many women reported that their husbands' attitudes increased the difficulties of both marriage and stepmothering. I sincerely believe that most of us do the best we can in any given situation depending on what we know at the time. But my experience as a psychotherapist, friend, mother, stepmother, and wife has led me to conclude that many of us need some intense training in the three major relationships discussed here: stepparenting, parenting, and marriage. No relationship is easy all of the time and each requires a strong commitment from both partners.

There are chemical and neurological differences between men and women, and male brains are generally less verbal and process emotional data more slowly than female brains. Yet I know that, with interest and desire, men can become excellent and insightful communicators. We are all vulnerable beings with strengths and short-comings, and we all need to be gentle with each other.

Many women, however, have been too gentle (or frightened) and have needed to become more adept in setting and sticking firmly to limits and boundaries in the area of relationship and intimacy. Often we have taken the easy way out and let our men off the hook. Both marriage partners need to accept equal responsibility for their relationship.

A Dramatic Example

Kim's case is pretty drastic, and her inability to set limits in her marriage caused her a great deal of pain. With emotion still shaking her voice after many years, Kim recalled when her husband's two daughters visited a month each summer. Although Peter was happy to see his girls, he did nothing to prepare for their visits, even though he worked part time and Kim worked full time. She said, "I got so anxious when they were coming it took all my energy just to keep up. I felt I had to entertain them and keep them happy and well fed, and I was always afraid their mother would make more trouble if they called saying they were bored or whatever. Plus, Peter's daughters always fought with each other, whereas my two girls didn't. It was so strained and chaotic when they were here, and Peter would never intervene or talk to them about anything."

Another issue, this one the proverbial straw that broke the camel's back, came one summer when the girls returned from camp with mildewed clothes. Since the girls were leaving for home the next morning, Kim stayed up the entire night bleaching and washing the mildew out. "Why?" was my astounded question. "Because I was so afraid of Peter's ex. She always sent an inventory of the girls' things and demanded it all come back in perfect condition." Kim is much more assertive now, but I could identify with her inability to make her husband understand how she was feeling, because I also had difficulty conveying my feelings to Gene.

Selective Awareness and the Wimp

Unlike Peter, Gene was and is a very conscientious and involved father and stepfather. Our difficulties circled, instead, around Gene's selective awareness and my insecurity and lack of assertiveness. For several years I was a scapegoat and target for one of Gene's daughters and her behavior toward me was painful, to say the least. Although I tried to talk with Gene about my feelings and her actions, he couldn't believe what I said and consequently saw no need to intervene.

Instead of having the courage to speak through a huge metaphoric megaphone by setting stronger limits and honoring them, I wimped out. Partly, I feared disappointing Gene and making him feel sorry that he married me. But the biggest fear that kept me more or less silent was the fear that he would leave me—maybe not leave the house, but sever our bond by leaving emotionally.

During those dark days I leaned heavily on my sons for support, understanding, and love—too heavily, I now believe. Though Mike and Brett have long since forgiven me, I still get a catch in my throat and heart remembering how much I asked of them when they were so young.

Finally, with the help of two dear and trusted women friends, I gathered the courage to set a limit. My plan was to have Paige, Gene, and me meet while I outlined the specific things that made my own home feel like an enemy camp. As the time approached for our talk, I was calm because I had already decided what to do if this meeting proved fruitless. I loved Gene and wanted to be married to him for the rest of my life, but I also knew that continuing to live with the stress I was feeling might actually shorten my life. Although it would be financially and emotionally difficult, I was willing to live in a separate residence until Paige was eighteen and out of the house. Realizing I had another option beyond mere endurance made me stronger.

But, bless her honest heart, it was Paige who saved the day. When her dad asked, "You don't do those things, do you Pooh Bear?" she mumbled, "Yeah, sort of . . . " The situation and atmosphere didn't improve dramatically, but it improved enough to make it tolerable for me. And, since I felt stronger, I was better able to stand up for myself and stick by my limits and boundaries. Recalling this scene the other day, Paige said, "I never could lie to my dad!" Thank goodness.

At times we need to speak up, but at other times, actions speak louder than words. Whatever approach you choose, it is essential to keep Dad in the loop. The one person most important to us and to the family needs to be willing to listen and be supportive and understanding. If this is a difficult area, as it was for us, please give yourself the gift of therapy, a support group, or conflict-resolution training.

SHEDDING SERVITUDE

We teach others how to treat us. If you feel like the family servant, as I did when I dressed as a maid for our Christmas picture, you probably have taught your family to expect servitude from you—not consciously, of course, but simply from being a woman culturally programmed to identify herself in terms of service to others.

Although it's wonderful to be useful, it's far from wonderful to feel taken advantage of, so let's explore how we might be subtly training family members to take advantage of us. Not wanting to be the evil, nagging stepmother, do you let annoyances slide or do the majority of the housework just because it's easier than hounding your husband and kids for help? Faced with mountains of laundry, meals to plan, homework to supervise, and schedules to coordinate, do you leap into your Wonder Woman bracelets and attempt to juggle it all on your own and end up feeling resentful?

Resentment is a clear warning that something is wrong. It is important for all women, and stepmoms in particular, to heed these warnings. We need to become very aware of our feelings, check the source of our resentment, and then work toward righting what's wrong for us and bringing the household back into balance and harmony. Slipping into servitude and failing to work through resentment can rot the very roots of our relationships.

When pushed beyond our limits, each of us handles the stress in different ways. We may say nothing at all and take on the victim or martyr role, or we may rage and scream like a wild woman. Neither is constructive nor does it bring us the understanding or closeness we desire. If you're responding in either of those ways—or in any other destructive manner—ask yourself this question: "What am I afraid of right now?" I usually answer that question with the single word "rejection." Fear of rejection kept me from shedding my servant status for a long while. Of course, allowing my fear to keep me quiet meant that I was rejecting my *own* feelings and rights—a Catch-22 for many of us "useful" women.

Paula, whose own children were grown when she became a stepmother, found a way to retire as the resident drudge after all attempts to neaten up her husband and his daughter failed. "I was at the height of a career I loved and didn't have the time or inclination to clean up after two slobs," she said. "So, I hired a housekeeper. It was great, because then we could relate to each other without my being a nag and them feeling guilty." Of course, Paula knew that not everyone can hire help but emphasized the importance of taking care of yourself. "I would advise stepmothers to make it as physically easy on themselves as possible. Housework, cooking, errands, driving—all that stuff. The emotional part is hard enough, so it's important to keep the other aspects of life as simple as possible!"

In our family, two of the kids were quintessential slobs, and the other two didn't exactly lose sleep over dust and dirt either. Gene is neat and tidy and a great house cleaner. I like order and cleanliness, but if I never touch another dust cloth, that'll be fine with me. One thing that did drive me crazy, however, was when the kids tossed anything and everything on the steps leading upstairs. Granted, the staircase was handy, the first thing you saw when entering the house, but it was also hazardous and messy. It's impossible to count the number of ineffective limits and threats I made to try and keep those darn stairs clear. Finally, tired of grumping about it, I'd periodically sweep everything into a box and stuff it in the closet.

Another stepmother hides things left strewn around and then charges the kids ten cents an item to reclaim their stuff. My way was to inform the kids what I was planning to do, tell them where the box would be, and then simply not respond to any further questions about missing stuff.

The Chains of Guilt and Shame

Nothing binds us to servitude more effectively than the feelings of guilt and shame that have been drilled into women's psyches for centuries. Guilt and shame are only appropriate as red lights warning us to stop. Stop thinking in self-destructive ways. Stop letting fear rule us. Stop devaluing ourselves. Or stop doing something unkind or inappropriate. Like a vaccine for a deadly disease, a little dose of guilt goes a long way, keeping us from uttering hurtful statements or telling us amends are needed. In larger doses, guilt or shame immobilize us.

We have both the wisdom and the power to break the chains of shame and guilt and become more loving, affectionate, and guilt-free women. Maya Angelou said, "A textured guilt was my familiar, my bed mate to whom I had turned my back. My daily companion whose hand I would not hold."[1] We can emulate this wise woman by turning our backs on both guilt and shame.

Affirmations are excellent tools for turning our backs on guilt and shame. One that I use repeatedly when side-swiped by self-castigating feelings is "I am a worthwhile and lovable woman even though I make mistakes." I may add the specific thing I'm feeling guilty about "I'm a worthwhile and loveable woman even though I said something that hurt So-and-so's feelings." Try creating a personal affirmation to counter your own particular brand of guilt or shame. Or, if the guilt and shame are pervasive and overwhelming, seek out a therapist who can help you move toward healing and inner freedom.

Accept Only Respect

No matter how deeply we hunger for emotional and spiritual well-being within our stepfamily circle, it will not exist without the all-important element of respect. Respecting someone means that we honor and value them while holding them in high esteem. With respect comes consideration of another person's feelings, attitudes, and vulnerabilities. Often we bestow respect on others but not on ourselves and, therefore, do not require others to treat us respectfully.

The habit of personal disrespect in not an easy one to break, but it can be done when we gently, and without judgment, observe our self-talk for signs of devaluing and blaming toward ourselves. Being aware of negative self-talk allows us to change it to a supportive, no-fault inner dialogue that bolsters self-respect and acceptance. For instance, when we hear our inner voice saying something disrespectful such as "I can't do *anything* right for these stepkids. I must be really stupid," we need to stop and say, "Whoa! That's not true." Then we can change the statement to a kind and considerate one such as, "This is a hard job, and I'm doing the best I can."

The same principle holds true when we begin accepting only respect from others. If, as a stepmom, you're given responsibility without respect or are expected to jump at the first demand from spoiled children or thoughtless adults, ask yourself if you feel respected. If the answer is no, stop! Refusing to be treated shabbily is necessary in earning the respect of others and teaching them to treat us well.

"Disrespect was the straw that almost crippled this camel," said stepmother Gloria as we sipped tea and compared stepping notes. Gloria went on to share that her stepchildren, poisoned by their mother's anger, treated her disrespectfully from the start of her relationship with their father. "They didn't speak to me when they first arrived on weekend stays; sometimes, they never spoke directly to me at all. If they did speak, it was to sneer at the food I served or a comment I made. It was pretty much hell for me."

Unable to change the kids' behavior or get across to her husband the extent of her anger, frustration, and pain, Gloria sought counseling with their minister. Guided by the observations and gentle proddings of their pastor, Gloria's husband began to understand that his "kids will be kids" attitude was driving a wedge between himself and his wife and not serving in the children's best interest either. With some reluctance, Gloria's husband agreed to insist that his children treat Gloria with respect.

With a small sigh, Gloria concluded, "It's better, Sue. The kids have mostly stopped being overtly disrespectful, and my husband is getting better and better at spotting disrespect and calling them on it. The best news is probably that *he* respects me more, and, consequently, I like him a lot more. We're still workin' on it."

As Gloria and many of us learn the hard way, respect is a nonnegotiable limit and boundary. When we become increasingly respectful of ourselves, free our servant selves from the shackles of guilt, shame, and "usefulness training," we become better equipped to train others to treat us respectfully and reasonably. Respected and freed from resentment we may choose how we want to be of service, allowing love to flow naturally and effortlessly from our hearts.

"If we are a family now, why do I feel so alone?" new stepmother Jody asked. Like many women who have never had children, Jody was shocked at how demanding and time consuming her husband's children were. "Sometimes I feel like an outsider in my own house when the kids are there," she continued. "My husband, Tom, and I don't even talk, and sex…Well, forget it. By the time that comes up, I'm so worn out and lonely that I could care less."

Jody learned it's easy to get lost in the shuffle and commotion when several new relationships come at once. In fact, you may be outnumbered if there are more people in your husband's family and, in that case, it's easy to feel overwhelmed and out of the loop yourself. Sometimes, faced with the demands of children and a love relationship, women shelve their own needs. With stepmothering, the changes can be so abrupt that we don't know what hit us until much later.

Luckily, we can count on our feelings to let us know when we've ignored our wants and needs and allowed ourselves to become lost, isolated, and overwhelmed. If you feel lost and isolated, in some ways you probably are. If you feel overwhelmed, very likely you've taken on too much and are feeling buried under the weight of the extra demands. But it's important to remember that only rarely do others in the family plot to isolate or overwhelm us; it just happens as a result of the circumstances. It's up to us to take care of ourselves by being aware of personal limits, honoring the feelings that arise, sharing them with our mate, and working together on ways to feel more included and less overwhelmed.

In some instances feelings of isolation and being overwhelmed represent unhealed wounds within us, and our stepfamilies are not the cause but merely the catalyst for our hurt. As an example, for the first few years of our marriage, I easily felt isolated, even abandoned, when Gene was particularly engrossed in his daughters. Sometimes I felt like the Little Match Girl, standing in the snow looking in on a warm familial scene. I was very conflicted about these feelings because I wanted Gene to be close to his girls. In fact, his interest in parenting was one of the things that I most loved about him. So, who was this selfish inner twit who felt jealous?

I decided to explore these feelings with a therapist. We discovered two inner aspects of myself that carried unhealed wounds from the past. My jealous feelings were held not by a twit but by an inner child who was quite aware that her baby sister, and only sibling, was her dad's favorite daughter. The other inner aspect was a young woman who still bled from double-edged betrayal —mentioned earlier—of her first husband falling in love with her best friend. These wounded voices within me insisted, and firmly believed, that men could not be counted on to love them and, even worse, feared that they were not lovable. Consequently, when Gene focused his attention on his daughters, my fears of loss and betrayal arose. Gene could have reassured me of his love until hell froze over but, until I transformed my own fears, they lurked within me waiting to pounce at the slightest hint of rejection or loss of interest.

If you find yourself wondering where certain feelings are coming from, it's helpful to ask, "Who's talking right now? Who is feeling this particular feeling? Who within me is reacting so strongly to this situation?" As I did, you may very well find an inner little girl or young woman who needs your love, support, and acceptance. We can often provide the needed solace for our inner selves by ourselves, but there may be times when the help of a compassionate professional would be beneficial.

If you are feeling more overwhelmed than isolated, take inventory of both the inner and outer responsibilities you have shouldered. Are they too much? Do you need to prioritize and decide what you need to cut? Are you allowing your space to be invaded? Is resentment pulling the plug on your energy reserves? If you're nodding in agreement, please be a gentle friend to yourself and set limits and boundaries that allow you to take care of yourself in the best way possible given your individual situation.

I heard some very creative suggestions from stepmoms concerning self-care. One has a special place in her garden in which she can vent anger by smashing glass jars. Another writes her complaints or pains on raw eggs and throws them against trees. Many women call friends for support and consolation. Beating the mattress with a tennis racket and going for brisk walks were also mentioned. Going to a movie is a favorite escape of mine. Discover what soothes you and clears your head and then give yourself permission to take care of yourself in those ways.

FREEING THE FIXER

One of the most important ways we can take care of ourselves is to realize that, while we are often the one best suited for the role of mediator between family members, we are neither the designated "savior" nor the responsibility "sponge." While we can be a helper and guide, each person in our family is responsible for his or her own life and feelings.

Many women have deep wells of compassion and understanding and unwittingly absorb and carry the feelings of an entire family. As a example, when Gene's youngest daughter, Lynnie, was a senior in high school, they had a very rough time with the separation/individuation dance. Striving to grow up and separate from Daddy, Lynnie became rebellious and more than a little moody. Gene tried handling her rebellion with tighter controls or statements such as, "Fine, then, move out..." Since they both have their fair share of German stubbornness, the righteous anger flowed freely between them. With my stomach tied in knots, I continually tried to "fix" the family by placating or soothing first one and then the other.

Guess what? Neither of them can remember that time very clearly, but I can. Why? Because I sopped up all of their feelings and carried them around in my own guts. Getting in the middle taught me how much I had to learn about staying out of other people's "stuff." This was Lynnie and Gene's transition to make, not mine.

It's so easy for us to run around collecting feelings and emotions that don't belong to us. The following technique, taught to me by my spiritual mother, Annabelle, has helped me deal with my tendency to collect feelings that don't belong to me. When struggling with intense feelings, ask your wise inner self or The Divine, "Are these *my* feelings that I am experiencing right now? If they are, I ask that I understand their origin and the lessons inherent in them. If they are *not* mine, I ask that they be taken by angels to the perfect, right place and transformed and transmuted into the perfect, right energy. I ask to be freed from that which is not mine." I have used this exercise with amazing results in many situations. Unfortunately, I forgot it during most of that year of struggle between Lynnie and Gene!

For your own well-being as well as your entire family, it's important to learn to say "no" with both courage and compassion. With practice and commitment, taking care of ourselves and setting self-nurturing limits can become second nature. Cultivating the ability to say "no" to unreasonable responsibilities and expectations makes it easier for us to say "yes" to love and laughter.

Give yourself permission to take steps to free the "fixer," who carries everyone's feelings, tries to make everything all right all the time, and does too much with too little reward. Transform wounded inner aspects of yourself by looking at places within you that need healing, and keep your husband in the loop. Taking these valuable steps will help you relax, enjoy, and learn from the stepmothering journey.

Moving To Higher Ground

When one is a stranger to oneself then one is estranged from others too. If one is out of touch with oneself, then one cannot touch others.

—ANNE MORROW LINDBERGH

When we are "in the trenches" as stepmothers, it's difficult to keep our sights on the big picture of love, commitment, and wholeness. Internally and externally we are busy, busy, busy.

Distanced by busyness from our soul's vision, we can lose track of our own lives, our purpose, goals, and dreams. To reclaim abandoned parts of ourselves and gain a soul perspective on the wholeness of our lives and loves, every now and then—for ten minutes, several hours, or several days—we need to move to higher ground: to retreat in order to rest, replenish, and touch the center of our souls.

One day while feeling especially busy and overwhelmed, I retreated to my bedroom and wrote this little allegory in my journal. "Gone to a tree branch like a waiting hawk. From my perch, I can see the wider vista of soul's scenery. Here I rise above my human emotions and reactions and touch heaven. Here, also, *they* can not reach me. Here, I safely wait... Patiently watching to see what, if anything, needs to be done or said."[Someone knocks on the door and I, Sue, tell them to go away, I'll be with them later.] "Interrupted, I flex one large sharp talon, swivel my head, and impale the intruder with a black beady eye."

Writing this piece in my journal helped me rise to a higher and more empowered place within myself. From my make-believe branch, I gained perspective about the issue I was upset over, no longer felt victimized by it, and, consequently, was able to resolve it amiably. Can you find a way to adapt this visioning process to work for you? What helps you soar to the higher ground of your good, true, and beautiful soul-self? One stepmom gathers an internal council of elders to guide her. Another takes a meditative walk in the mountains. For these women, learning to become open and spacious has proved to be an extraordinary help in dealing with step-mothering challenges.

Opening To Spaciousness

Being nervous, uptight, or anxious causes us to constrict physically, emotionally, and mentally. If you've ever gone into a job interview or an exam fully prepared and then been overcome by anxiety, you know what it's like to have everything you know squeezed right out of your mind. The same is true of emotions. When we are consumed by pain or confusion, everything seems to compress around the anxiety and resultant turmoil. Becoming rigid and tightly focused on the object of our animosity causes clenched jaws, guts, and hearts. When we're clamped in such a vise, all that is clear-headed and compassionate within us is squished right out. Constantly fixing our attention on our anger, helplessness, and resentment closes and embitters our hearts.

None of us wants to have a closed, bitter, and constricted heart. We yearn to be open-hearted and compassionate women. The good news is that, with a little practice, we can become the spacious and unlimited beings we were meant to be, sometimes simply by inviting openness and expansion to replace tightness and constriction within us.

Although opening into spaciousness may sound complex or mysterious, it's really very simple. Let me give you an example that Nirmala, a Buddhist stepmother, shared with me: "I am familiar with the meditation practice of using my breath to create spaciousness within my body. So when my stepson does something irritating and I notice that my jaws are locked tightly by my frustration, I excuse myself. Going to my room with the intention to let go, I close my eyes and invite my breath into my jaws first and then into my entire body. I imagine that the inflow and outflow of my breath are ocean waves tenderly washing the negative emotions from me. With each deepening breath, I visualize my heart expanding until it feels as vast as the ocean. If I'm especially angry or upset, I may pray that angels or the Buddha help open the places within me where I feel the most strangled. Depending on the circumstances, this exercise may take three minutes or thirty minutes. But it's time well spent because, from a spacious self, I can deal with my stepson lovingly and firmly. Plus, I can look at myself in the mirror and say, 'Well done' afterwards."

For Nirmala, big dividends come with her ability to break out of the cocoon of constriction and open into spaciousness. She and her stepson are forging a close bond and he views her as a trusted friend.

We don't have to be either a Buddhist or a practiced meditator to become more open and spacious. Breath and imagination are all we need. And the wonderful thing about softening and opening is that it can be done anywhere at any time, *and* it is miraculously effective.

I am neither a Buddhist nor do I meditate daily—even though my yearly New Year's resolutions always include the desire to do so—but I regularly use breathing and visualization to open my heart or to release my body and mind when I'm worried or anxious. The other night, for instance, I was sleepless with concern over one of our adult kids. It usually works for me to pray, surround them with light, and ask their guardian angels to protect them. But that hadn't helped. Taking inventory, I noticed that my stomach ached and my heart felt like a stone.

Time to breath and open. I imagined that my breath was warm buttery light and invited it deeply into my belly and heart. The next thing I knew it was morning.

Spaciousness softens our tense grip on whatever worries us and allows us to open to the peace that yearns to flood our being. You, too, can breathe, imagine, and open to the comfort and clarity of spaciousness.

RETREATING TO REST AND REPLENISH

Although we may be exasperated if our car battery dies, we don't usually kick, scream, and demand that the car get up and get going. Nor do we push the car to our planned destination. Although we may bargain with the battery to "just take us to this final meeting or soccer game and we'll let you rest," or we may try to make it feel guilty by scolding—"How can you do this to me right now? Don't you care how important this outing is?"—we do so with tongue firmly planted in cheek. Fully aware that there are only a few options to the dead battery problem, we accept the predicament and choose the handiest solution: getting a jump start from someone close by, calling AAA, or buying a new battery.

So, what do you do when your personal battery begins to weaken? Unfortunately, we often fail to listen to the physical, emotional, mental, and spiritual parts of ourselves when they warn us that we are running out of energy. In effect, many of us get out and push a self whose battery is faltering, if not already dead. To take care of ourselves, we need to heed those messages. When we pause and truly listen to ourselves, we will know when it is time to rest and restore.

Taking Care of Ourselves

Taking care of ourselves means that we must not only listen to the warnings from our inner selves, but also honor and act on them. In other words, when we are exhausted, we need to rest. If we are depressed or mentally unbalanced, we need to find the feelings at the root of the symptoms and work—probably with help—toward healing and transforming them. Granted, there is rarely an opportune time for taking a break, but it is crucial for our own well-being as well as for those we care about that we do take a break when we need it.

In her late forties, Joyce, a dear friend of mine, met and married the man of her dreams. The only catch was that he lived on one coast and she lived on the other. With grave misgivings but good intentions, Joyce sold her house, uprooted her psychotherapy practice, and left her adult children and grandchild to be with her beloved and near his adult children. I visited a few months after she moved and was shocked by her lifelessness. My bright, enthusiastic friend had become quiet, medicated, and washed out.

Months later she realized that to really thrive she needed to live in California and be nearer her children.

"I was willing to compromise in many ways. I would live anyplace in California where my husband, Paul, could find work that he liked. I was even willing to be married and commute to be with him." What made her realize both the cause and cure for her depression? "I looked in the mirror one day and saw a lethargic old woman. I was so shocked that I said aloud, 'Who *are* you?'" Without dramatics, she added, "I finally let myself see that I would die if I stayed where I was."

Joyce's story shows how easily we ignore our inner cries for rest and restoration. Even as a trained therapist, it took her a long time, and a bout with severe depression, to become aware that her soul needed California and easy access to her children to reclaim its former vitality. For her husband's sake, she *wanted* it to be okay to live on the East Coast. But it wasn't. Thankfully, she took action that her husband honored and agreed to.

What Replenishes You?

Women come in different makes and models. What replenishes one's battery will deplete another's. As an example, Emily, a stepmother of three, recharges her battery by attending a two-week summer camp with forty other women. They sleep outside on the ground, bathe in the pond, cook over an open fire, and do ceremonies until late at night. She loves it. "I come back refreshed, grounded, and ready to tackle the next round of family stuff," she enthused.

While the camaraderie sounds fun, the accommodations make me cringe. I'm an indoor-sleeping kinda gal. Therefore, when most of the kids were teenagers and my emotional reserves hit empty or below, I would take myself to a nearby motel for a night or two. Usually, I spent the first few hours writing furiously in my journal and releasing pent-up tears of frustration and sadness. When the catharsis was complete, I would rent a movie, call a friend, eat take-out food, write poetry, meditate, or sleep. Running away from home was just rebellious enough to feel heavenly.

Some stepmothers find their work restorative. Asked what she does to take care of herself, Peggy, also a psychotherapist said, "I love my work. It helps me remember who I am." When I was in private practice, I, too, found it energizing to go to my office and assume an identity that had nothing whatsoever to do with being a mother, stepmother, or wife. There I was my professional self, Sue the psychotherapist.

For some women, massage is a wonderful antidote to both physical and emotional stress. Relaxing under the ministering hands of an accomplished masseuse can be a nurturing way to learn to receive and accept. We are touched, soothed, and pampered without anything being asked of us. Not only a luxury, massage is conducive to both mental and physical health, since it encourages us to be vulnerable and open to the sensations of our bodies and souls. If you haven't already, allow yourself to try massage and see if you might find it as healing as I do.

I encourage you to find a few quiet moments and list what is restful and restorative to you. Friends, movies, gardening, rock climbing, conversation, taking classes, sewing, baking, backpacking, meditating, listening to or playing music, exercising—if it recharges your battery and is financially feasible, anything is okay.

When we are depleted because of pain, confusion, or exhaustion, we are incapable of absorbing or accepting any more input. If we try to ignore or push through our depletion, our output is unreliable and can even become destructive. For the good of ourselves and all those with whom we relate, it's both wise and loving to retreat and replenish ourselves when fatigued, drained, or burned out.

SANCTUARY OF SOLITUDE

Too much of almost everything bombards us every day. Noise, for instance, is everywhere. "Music" surrounds shoppers and store clerks, traffic constantly dins against city ears, radios blare from cars and portable boom boxes, and phones ring endlessly. Do I even need to mention the normal noise and pandemonium that exist in a home bustling with children and/or teenagers? Everywhere we turn, our senses are assailed and over-stimulated. The hubbub of daily life can be exhilarating, but in our hearts, we know that balance between activity and quiet is important. How and where can we find that place of balance and quiet?

Becoming Reacquainted with Self

While external noise grates on our nerves and exhausts us, it is the unexamined inner cacophony of criticism, doubt, and confusion that really takes a toll on our sense of self. Sometimes we need to drop all the balls we're juggling and retreat into the sanctuary of solitude in order to understand ourselves better and reestablish inner harmony. Embracing periods of quietness and solitude is a necessity for our mental and physical health and for the evolution of our dreams and talents. In solitude, we can become reacquainted with our true selves.

Once, feeling buried under layers of family demands and personal pressure, I took a popular self-help book and escaped to a funky little cabin near the beach. My goal was twofold: to find out who I was outside the roles I played and to understand why I felt so restless and resentful much of the time. I remember throwing that book against the fireplace in frustration and wailing, "Yes, yes, I *know* what's wrong with me. Now, how do I change it?" Impulsively, I vowed, "If I ever write a book, I'm going to concentrate on making it helpful and encouraging!"

Until that moment, I'd never considered writing as a career. In fact, my experiences in English classes had been discouraging. Although I kept a journal and sprinkled words on pages and called them poems, I would never in a million years have called myself a writer. Even though I pushed it away, the idea of writing kept surfacing; partial concepts floated by as I washed dishes, yellow legal pads became my constant companions, and flashes of inspiration woke me in the middle of the night.

In a sanctuary of solitude, amid the quiet of my own energy, I moved to higher ground, became less of a stranger to myself, and discovered who I wanted to become above and beyond my roles as mother, stepmother, wife, and therapist. On retreat from my everyday world and freed from excessive external stimuli, my passion for writing revealed itself—a passion that brings me much joy and continues to burn brightly after many years.

Creating a Mini-Retreat

It isn't necessary to go away for days to different locales, but finding ways to move apart from both our families and society in mini-retreats is essential. In the first months after our stepfamily merged, I, being a night owl, stayed up many nights to watch the moon rise and set while pouring my feelings into my journal. Another stepmother, Rachel, uses the early morning hours as her time alone. "I get up at 5:30 before anyone else is stirring. In the blessed quiet, I make a cup of tea and sit in the kitchen and watch the sun come up. Sometimes I pray or meditate, but mostly I just soak in the peace and think my own thoughts." Rachel went on to say that she feels it is this solitary hour that somehow fills her and allows her to remain fairly easygoing and flexible throughout the day.

No matter what form your sanctuary of solitude takes, it can provide the place where you connect most deeply with yourself. And, of course, you are the person with whom you most need to be in touch. To honor our individuality and uncover what is yearning to express itself within us, we need to understand our feelings and listen to ourselves with love. Within your inner being is an eternal spring. Go there to be renewed and refreshed.

～⚭～

The complexity of stepmothering exacts a heavy toll unless you take good and gentle care of yourself. Give yourself the gift of quiet time to open into spaciousness, to rest and replenish, to discover and cherish who you most deeply are. Doing so can open your heart and encourage love to flow more freely from you. Be kind to yourself, and grant yourself permission to relax and rejuvenate in the sanctuary of solitude. Retreating to rest, replenish, and process feelings gives your soul a chance to catch up with your body. Together, body and soul, can meet any challenge. Choosing to move to higher ground amid challenges helps us to grow our souls and reclaim lost parts of ourselves while continuing to lovingly care for our families and stepfamilies. Being in touch with our true selves allows us to truly touch others.

PART FOUR

Strengthening Your Marriage

For one human being to love another: that is perhaps the
hardest of all our tasks, the ultimate, the last test and proof,
the work for which all other work is but preparation.

—RAINER MARIA RILKE

We are stepmothers for one reason and one reason only:
we love the father of these children. In the fullness of
time, we may also grow to love the children, but that is
not our first priority. Next to caring for ourselves, loving
our man and strengthening our marriage are of primary
importance. As the poet Rilke emphasizes, love is not
easy. And love that comes with a ready-made family is
even more difficult. Therefore, we need to faithfully
make time to rekindle our love and remember why we
married.

We all want our marriages to survive and thrive and,
to insure that they do, we need to make a conscious commitment to the challenge of caring for and nurturing our
union. While children can bring us closer, they can also
create divisive chasms. It is in the best interest of all to
first build a joyful and stable relationship with our husbands and then invite the children to join in. Children
crave the security and modeling of a companionable and

cohesive partnership. Your unity as a couple, as well as your commitment to yourself as an individual, will be a tremendous boon in helping the kids develop into caring and self-confident adults.

At its best, marriage is a sacred partnership between equals, a deep friendship that brings us sanctuary, soul growth, and sizzle. We have a deep and holy hunger for sacred partnership. Love is hard work, but it is also the work for which we were created. And a stepfamily gives us ample opportunity to hone our loving skills. Yet we always need to remember that as stepmothers, our fundamental task, first and foremost, is to protect the sanctity of our unions and to strengthen the marriage bonds shared with our husbands. With that strong and loving union supporting us, we will be able to reach out and share more gently, compassionately, and lovingly with those around us.

Marriage Is For Good Friends

Friendship is a sheltering tree.

—SAMUEL TAYLOR COLERIDGE

In a stepfamily, the branches of the family tree are immediately alive with the insistent calling of baby birds. Have you ever walked by a tree where baby birds are letting their parents know they're hungry? Do their relentless, raucous, demanding cries sound familiar? Often we barely have time to take a deep breath, let alone forge a solid and sheltering friendship with our beloved, before children—his and often ours—are busily and noisily making their wants and needs known. Before the roots of our marital friendships can sink deeply into the ground, our children require attention and energy from us.

Whatever love and attraction drew us to our mate in the first place, it is friendship that will keep us together and help us weather the rough times. Friendships, like trees, start from little seeds and, with care and nourishment, grow into safe and sheltering havens. For friendships to ripen as they mature, consistent love and attention are required. And that's the rub. With children involved in our relationship from the start, we need to be extra vigilant about guarding our commitment to pay loving attention to each other or the children's needs will take precedence, leaving our friendship stunted.

Eileen and her husband, Steve, were teachers in the same school and good friends before they married. However, under the pressure of combining six children and then adding one of their own, during their first several years together, "Stress ruled!" Eileen said, "We just worked and tried to manage the kids, money, and all the other stuff." She explained that their friendship was a vague but sustaining memory during those early years and then added with a smile, "*Now*, with all but one kid gone, we're working on getting reconnected, becoming close, and having the relationship we want."

Asked what she would do differently if she had it to do over again, Eileen said, "I would be much more committed to taking care of myself and making time for Steve and me." She added with a rueful laugh, "I'd be wiser." Wouldn't we all?

As Eileen and Steve discovered, it isn't easy to nourish an already existing friendship while coping with the demands from children and life in general. And, I learned it is also difficult to grow an embryonic friendship. Gene and I were madly in love when we married, but our friendship was still a seedling that needed consistent care and nurturing. Most often we managed to be good caretakers, but, at times when we were caught in the grip of fear, ignorance, or righteousness, we brought out our emotional buzz saws.

I believe several things sustained us during those painful outbursts. First, we're essentially nice people whose souls seemed to recognize each other when we first met. Second, although we were vulnerable, we were also strong and capable individuals and I, especially, was working hard on being my own good friend. Third, and probably the key factor, we both had a deep and abiding commitment to making our marriage work and to creating a rich and rewarding life together. We wanted our relationship to provide the sanctuary of friendship, a sheltering tree during both stormy and sunny skies.

CONSCIOUS COMMITMENT IS THE CORNERSTONE

A commitment is a pledge or promise. What do we want to commit to our beloved and to his children? What commitments do we promise to keep to ourselves and our own children? These are extremely important questions to ask, because your family is founded upon the answers.

The structure of marriage and family rests on the cornerstone of commitment, and the strength of our commitment determines the strength, durability, and happiness of ourselves, our beloved, and all the children. Without the commitment to love, honor, respect, and cherish your mate, as well as the commitment to treat all the children with unfailing kindness and respect, sacred partnership cannot exist. Only when shored up by an unfailing commitment to care for each other as much as we care for ourselves can we create the sheltering tree of friendship and enduring love for which we all yearn.

When asked, "What kept you going?" most stepmothers listed commitment as the foundation of their relationship. Long-term stepmom Teri was a good example. "Commitment, with a capital C!!!" she said, then chuckled, "In fact, we used to say to each other, 'The first one who quits gets *all five* kids!'" Wisely Teri added, "I constantly reminded myself of the big picture. When we were forty, fifty, and so on, I wanted to be with *this* man and have all the kids home for Christmas." When things were tough—and they regularly were—and her commitment wavered, Teri remarked, "I looked at Joel and remembered he was the best man I knew and then reminded myself that it was all about *us* and not so much about the kids." Last year all of the kids celebrated Christmas at Teri and Joel's house. "It was great to have them all," she said, "and equally great when they all left!"

While commitment is the cornerstone of marriage, we need to be judicious and make our commitments only to a man with whom we can comfortably keep them, a man we truly want as a lover and friend, one to whom we can say without reservation, "I am here through hell and high water."

Motives for Marrying

It's my experience that our motives for marriage are often a mixed bag. Some are based wholly on love and respect. Others are more selfish and/or primitive. I had many reasons for marrying Gene. The first was that I had fallen head over heels in love and believed with all my heart that the five falling stars we saw on the night we met were a sign that we were destined to be together. Less admirable, were my relief at finding a responsible man and my desire to be taken care of and "rescued" from the exhaustion of single parenthood and the anxiety of borderline poverty. I saw him as my security blanket and expected him to shoulder all of the financial responsibility. He, in turn, expected me to provide the emotional shelter for all six of us while he was "top dog" in terms of decision making. In those days, equal we were not.

Gene fulfilled the sheltering tree and knight on a white horse role beautifully. But we sat on the back porch of hell a few years later when I became restive with my one-down role and needed to grow up, assert my independence, and become an equal partner. Thankfully, we made it through those fires without being severely charred, just decidedly singed. However it would have been far less painful if I had been honest with myself and Gene early on about my take-care-of-me motives.

I wish I had been able to say, "I love you madly and feel very blessed that you love me too. But there is also a part of me that is extremely weary and yearns for you to take care of me and my sons." With my tacit expectation out in the open, we could have had a dialogue about what this expectation meant to both of us and what he might expect in return for his care and support. But back then we were too awash in the euphoria of new love and idealism to notice much beyond our joy at finding each other.

Eventually reality hit and with it came the need to speak of our unacknowledged motives and to begin to reshape our relationship. Ask yourself if your motives for marrying were based on love or unconscious fears and needs. As Gene and I needed to do, it is never too late to ferret out motives and intentions that may be undermining your ability to make a clear and committed choice to be fully present in your marriage and to your partner. It's also never too late to change your motives and intentions if you desire to do so. We did, and so can you, if your marriage is built on a firm base of love and commitment.

A bond not tethered to a deep commitment will break under the strain of stepmothering, so for the sake of all involved, I urge you to examine your motives for marriage. If this is difficult for you to do alone, please find a wise friend and/or therapist to help you uncover and examine your motivation for being in the relationship. You may find motives that were once viable and even valuable that now need to be transformed in the alchemy of awareness and fresh intention. And this is as it should be, since all vital and alive friendships evolve, change, and grow.

Revamping and Restructuring

If you discover that you had questionable motives for marrying, or if your marriage simply feels a little stale, all is not lost. A good marriage is a flexible one, and it's definitely possible to revamp and restructure it to one you can happily recommit to. Ask yourself, "What motives did we have for marriage that now need to be revamped and updated? Have we slipped into a routine where only the issues that itch the most get scratched or the commitments that cry the loudest get heard?" If only itching issues and crying commitments get our attention, my bet is they center around our children rather than ourselves and our relationship with our mate. Are we still excited and interested in our love and life with our husband, or does our friendship need an infusion of energy?

Shortly before their tenth anniversary Dionne suggested to his wife, Randi, "Let's send your kids to your mom and my kids to my mom and go away for a weekend within the next couple of months. I want us to think of this as a reorganization of our family corporation." Intrigued, Randi asked what prompted his idea. "Well, not to hurt your feelings or anything, but I think we're in a rut. We need a new vision and new goals for our relationship, and I want to do it before our tenth anniversary."

At the time of Dionne's proposal, Randi confessed that she felt so exhausted that even a weekend away felt like yet another obligation, another duty. Not having the energy to do anything but agree to his plan, she said yes and three weeks later they went away together. "It was absolutely the best thing that we've ever done for our relationship. Dionne made all of the arrangements for the kids and for the hotel and insisted that the first day was only for resting. Randi said "Then, like the good manager that he is, he sat us down to make a game plan for revitalizing our marriage and making the 'bottom line' more attractive to us both."

Although many wonderful relationship perks came from their revamping weekend, the most important thing to Randi was the feeling of being cared for that came from it. Dionne's willingness to spend so much thought, energy, and expense to create a time and space in which they could think and plan only about themselves as individuals and as a couple helped Randi reclaim her awareness of what a great couple they were.

Randi and Dionne now take one evening a month to look exclusively at their relationship, talk about how they might like things to change, and compliment each other on parts of their lives together that are working exceptionally well. With a grin, Randi said, "You might say we take our marriage temperature every month. It's amazing how much easier hard stuff is when I know that we have that monthly meeting set to discuss it all. I now believe, beyond a shadow of a doubt, that we will be a great old couple long after this daily stepfamily stuff is over."

Change is an inevitable part of all living things and our relationships are no exceptions. When Dionne realized something was lacking in his marriage, he put his business acumen to work and came up with a plan in which he and Randi could address, brainstorm, and often solve the issues and situations that undermined their love and friendship.

In my case, when my take-care-of-me approach to our marriage began to pinch, I needed to revamp it into a let's-be-equal-partners stance. Then both of us restructured our relationship to support the kind of friendship we now wanted and the partnership we were capable of. I needed to grow up, take some financial responsibility, and insist upon equality in our relationship. Gene needed to relinquish some control and let go of his fantasy of having a geisha girl for a wife. In essence, we realized it was time to make a different commitment and mature into the sacred partnership appropriate for the man and woman we were and the woman and man we wanted to become.

THE ART OF OPENHEARTED LOVING

Absolutely nothing is more strengthening to a marriage than a sincere desire to live and love from an open heart. Making a commitment to open our hearts amid the confusion of stepparenting may sometimes seem downright scary and the last thing in the world we feel like doing.

But love is not a feeling, love is a decision. Practicing the art of openhearted living is something that we can decide to do, minute by minute, day by day.

At the very core of our being, we long for meaningful and heartfelt connection with our chosen mate. The very essence of our being holds a deep desire to live compassionate, caring lives and yearns for the genuine solace of a sheltering friendship. Nowhere is this desire to return to openheartedness more intense than in our primary relationships. Nowhere is the need for kindness and consideration more keenly felt than in the family circle.

Francine, a stepmother to four live-in children, told me in all seriousness, "There should be sainthood for all stepmothers." *Where do we sign up?* Seriously, I do believe that fulfilling the role of stepmother gives us a unique opportunity to create more love and openheartedness in the world. It's easy—perhaps even a biological imperative—to love the children who come to life under our own hearts, but it's not always effortless to open our hearts to the children who come to us as part of our marriage package.

As stepmothers, we can help bring more love into the world by opening our arms and hearts to ourselves, our husbands, and all of the children involved. By no means does this mean that we need to feel lovey dovey with all the kids, all the time. Nor with our husbands either, for that matter. Not at all. But it does mean making a conscious commitment to live from our hearts as much as possible, a commitment that includes choosing to return to our hearts when we notice that we've drifted away from heart-centered loving.

While mystics, poets, and philosophers have known for eons that love is the healer of all wounds and a balm for all that ails us, scientists are beginning to agree. For several years now the power of the heart has been measured in scientific laboratories like the Institute of HeartMath in Boulder Creek, California. The Institute's studies provide compelling evidence that activating heart energy harmonizes the body/mind connection, reduces stress, and increases well-being physically, emotionally, mentally, and spiritually. In my own life, I've had many chances to activate heart energy and watch with joy as it helped harmonize the man/woman connection between Gene and me and the woman/child connection between me and my sons and stepdaughters.

Our heart is the seat of our soul, the abiding place of our essence. Our hearts embody wisdom and compassion. Deeply intuitive, they know what is loving and nurturing and understand the bonds that connect us to both our beloved and The Beloved. Becoming openhearted not only helps us become more loving but following our hearts can also lead to fulfillment, peace of mind, increased creativity, and better health.

Our bodies themselves affirm the appropriateness of self-love and care; our physical hearts pump oxygen-rich blood to the heart itself *first*, before blood goes out to other areas of the body. If nourishing itself first is good for the very seat of our soul, doesn't it make sense that loving and caring for ourselves is also a worthy—even spiritual—goal? As modeled by our actual heart, taking care of ourselves makes us more loving and better able serve those with whom we are in relationship.

How to Open Our Hearts

We know our hearts are open when relating to others seems effortless and laughter dances easily from our lips. We feel free and in the flow. Energetically, we may feel like a stream happily bubbling from its source. Like water, love wants to flow naturally and freely.

But held captive in a closed heart, love becomes grabby, then leaden and heavy with attachment and dependence. When our hearts are tightly shut, we feel constricted and limited, anxious and suspicious, resentful and overwhelmed. I certainly know the feeling, and I bet you do too.

Fear is usually the cause of our closedheartedness. For our hearts to open, we need to bring our fear into the light of awareness and learn to protect our hearts from harm. Over time, I have found several helpful ways for transforming fear and opening my heart. For example, I have wrestled with the fear of rejection for as many years as I can remember, and though it no longer paralyzes me as it once did, it does rear up occasionally, especially in my relationship with Gene. A few months ago, he and I went through a rough patch when each of our hearts seemed locked away. We treated each other as cool acquaintances, not openhearted friends. I knew that I needed to gather the courage to initiate a very honest conversation and set some limits and boundaries, but I was scared spitless to do so. Fear yapped at me: *Things could get even worse. You might be driven even farther apart and never come back together . . .* Help!

In order to get back in touch with my heart, I talked over my fears with a friend, prayed and meditated quite a lot, visualized the hands of Christ and the Mother Mary protecting my heart from harm, and made a conscious decision to send Gene little surges of love from a safe distance. I also told Gene I'd be needing to talk soon but was not ready yet. I continued reassuring myself that I was safe and strong and affirmed that our marriage was sound. Whenever I remembered, I breathed the love of God into my heart and then breathed it out toward both me and Gene. This was not a quickie-fix. It took me several days of "pumping to myself first" before I could count on my heart remaining open when we talked.

Happily, we both arrived at an emotional place where we could talk from the heart and have a conversation that helped us better understand each other as we moved through the crisis to a higher and deeper connection. If we had confronted each other with our hearts barricaded closed, I have no doubt that the same talk would have ended much differently.

It's not always easy to determine if we're acting from our hearts or reacting from fear or an old habit. A few good questions to ask are, "Does this come from my heart? Will I look in the mirror and admire the person I see there if I continue on this track? What am I afraid of right now?" Just for the fun of it, I sometimes ask, "What would a saint do in this situation?"

Cultivating openheartedness requires us to become more acutely aware of our hearts. I, myself, use several deceptively simple ways to do this. First, I simply remember my heart and its capacity for love, focus on it, and gently ask it to open. Second, putting my hand over my heart and gently thanking it for its continual, life-giving work and asking for its guidance can bring profound changes in my actions, attitudes, and feelings. Third, in an uncomfortable situation, it's wonderfully centering for both wife and husband to pause and consciously return to their hearts. Simply stop and put one hand on your heart and one hand on your husband's heart, then—silently or aloud—ask to speak from the wisdom of your heart and let the love between you be your guide. It is powerfully transformative to take a moment to focus on opening our hearts, and remember the love that brought us together.

Very importantly, the art of openhearted loving is meant to be practiced on ourselves as well as others. Yoga class is a great place for me to keep my heart open to myself. How might you practice openhearted loving toward yourself by treating yourself in ways that fill and restore you?

The role of stepmother offers us many opportunities to practice openheartedness. The next time you feel your heart closing, try a little experiment. Put your hand on your heart and reassure it that you will keep it safe and will not abandon it. Imagine that you are breathing the love of the Divine into your heart and allowing that love to flow through you to the person or situation you are dealing with. At the very least, you will feel more calm and centered. At best, the entire predicament may be defused.

A Safe Haven

Each of us needs and deserves a safe haven, a place where we are welcomed, supported, and treated with kindness, a place where we are *valued*. When the frenzy of the world or the frustrations of the family become intense, we need to regroup within the sanctuary of a safe place and/or within the arms of a friendly person. Ideally, our mate can be that person and our home that place. Even though a home teeming with children rarely feels like a sanctuary of quiet and calm, it can be a safe haven when we and our husbands are dear, trusted, and openhearted friends.

Good friends never wound those they love on purpose. They take to their hearts the physician's credo: "First, do no harm." We all need physical and emotional safety if we are to be free to reveal the person we truly are and become the person we are destined to be. And only in a safe and secure environment will our marriage flourish. The more openhearted we are, the safer we will be and the safer others will be in our presence. We all know when we're not safe in a relationship, and we protect ourselves by closing down or jumping on the offensive. We try appeasing our mate in order to keep the peace or aggressively attempt to gain control of the relationship. Neither will create a safe haven.

Living in a safe haven helps us soar to our highest potential. But if we crash, compassion, encouragement, and solace cushion our fall. Knowing that our beloved is *with* us, never against us, surrounds us with the solace of safety. Each of us will stumble and fall, especially in our unfamiliar roles as stepparents. That is why it's such a comfort to walk hand in hand with an openhearted friend on whom we can rely.

Appreciation, Approval, and Applause

While talking to a couple about stepmothering, Fred complimented his wife on raising his three children, "I just call her Leslie, the Rock!" he said fondly. Such appreciation, approval, and applause is the mark of an openhearted, secure friendship and gives the recipient the incentive and energy to keep on keeping on.

All gardeners know that their plants and flowers bloom and bear fruit more readily when they are carefully and tenderly nurtured, fertilized, and blessed by enough light. Like plants, we need to be nurtured by appreciation, fertilized with approval, and applauded in the light of friendship. When showered with these life-enhancing gifts, we flower into the persons we are meant to be. Deprived of appreciation, approval, and applause, our energy is depleted and we wither on the vine.

This morning I harvested a ripe tomato from a plant in my backyard. Inadvertently, I also broke a vine leading to two small green tomatoes. Although I left them hanging there by a slim tendril, they may not ripen because the vine that supplies their nutrients has been damaged. My tomato plant provides a good analogy for marriage. Although we may find applause, appreciation, and approval from sources outside our marriage, receiving them from our intimate relationships is as necessary to us as an undamaged vine is to a tomato. We are happiest when our openhearted friendship with our husband is a strong and sturdy vine that carries the nutrients we both need and desire.

Of course, what's good for one tomato is also good for the other. While everyone needs applause, approval, and appreciation, I've learned that men not only need these things, they crave them. Men like appreciation almost as much as they do sex. Without appreciation, men wilt, withdraw, or become overly critical. It's very important that we accept and honor what our men need. Fed with appreciation, approval, and applause, husbands ripen more readily into openhearted and affectionate friends.

If we want to be a pair of "hot tomatoes," we need to make a conscious commitment to keep the vine of our marriage openhearted and freely flowing with daily appreciation, unstinting approval for even the smallest things, and enthusiastic applause at the drop of a hat. Get creative. How can you show your mate how much you love and appreciate him? Possibly a love note with a short list of you-done-goods, gold stars on his shorts in appreciation for a love-making session, a literal standing ovation where you jump to your feet and applaud when he shares a triumph, a thank-you note for those things you appreciated this week, a just-because-you're-you gift, maybe a special dinner without *any* kids, a back rub, or a candle-lit after-dinner treat for just you and your hot tomato. . . .

I've heard it said that "energy flows where attention goes." What an invaluable tip for strengthening our marriage and befriending our mate. Placing our attention on providing consistent appreciation, approval, and applause to those we love, not only focuses their energy on the good things about themselves but teaches them to return the favor to us. A complementary adage could be "attributes grow where attention flows." Those attributes that we applaud, appreciate, and approve of will grow as we reward them with positive attention.

Bringing Out the Best

One of the virtues of an openhearted marriage and friendship is that it brings out the best in those involved. Being able to say, "I am a better person because I am with you" is a wonderful blessing. Sometimes two people bring out the best in each other "automagically," as my friend Annabelle says, but most of the time we need to consciously create an atmosphere conducive to such growth.

Being openhearted, providing a safe haven, and generously giving appreciation and approval go a long way to bringing out the best in each other. And, in order to be her best self, a woman needs to feel secure. Perhaps as an instinctive desire to provide protection for our babies, we women need security to a far greater extent than do our men. Our well-being is directly proportional to our sense of security. When sustained by a sense of security within herself and in her partner's commitment to her and to their marriage, a woman can personify love and gentle nurturance.

Additionally, our relationships need to be free from sniping and snipping, criticism or put-downs, and any teasing that makes the recipient feel uncomfortable in any way. Mean-spirited teasing is a bastardized version of attack and as such is expressly forbidden. If you and your partner bring out the worst in each other, your relationship needs a profound overhaul, one that you probably cannot accomplish by yourself. Please, if you or your husband feel diminished in any way as a result of being together, run, don't walk, to a competent and compassionate professional!

Good friends and openhearted marriage partners support and complement each other. They invite their beloved to be who they truly are, they support each other at all times, and they magnify the "good stuff" within each other. They are each other's biggest fans.

Within the sanctuary of a gentle, supportive, and committed marriage, each of us finds the safe haven for which we yearn. And from that safety and security, we are encouraged to soar to heights never before imagined.

MARRIAGE IS FOR GROWN-UPS

During the demise of my first marriage, I saw the therapist who authored the book *Marriage Is for Grown-ups*. Talking with him, I came to realize that neither my first husband nor I had been mature grown-ups in our marriage. Granted, we married very young, but nonetheless our immaturity impacted many lives, most significantly our sons'.

As a thirty-year-old single mother, I took it upon myself to grow up. Therapy helped. Returning to graduate school and majoring in psychology was an incredible eye-opener and, thankfully, my grad school, while heavy on academics, was also very grounded in practicality.

My education has turned out to be a blessing for both my personal and professional lives. But probably the most important aspect to my maturation was a dogged determination to take responsibility for my own life, feelings, and actions. I was determined to free myself from the emotional chains that bound me and knew that not doing so would render me incapable of ever having an open-hearted, satisfying marriage based on mutuality and friendship.

By the time I met Gene at thirty-three, I had made some strides toward being a real grown-up, but I certainly had a ways to go—*still* have a ways to go, as do we all. Growing up is a life-long process, but we can choose to *act* with maturity a majority of the time.

Maturity is hardly the stuffy, stiff, unadulterated righteousness that we thought it was when we were kids. On the contrary, maturity actually brings increased freedom and tolerance, an openness to our own and other's foibles and points of view. Ideally, with maturity, the pressing need to be right diminishes and we gain a better perspective about what is and is not important in relationships. Equipped with a softer attitude and a wider viewpoint, we make more loving and thoughtful choices in relationships with our friends and family. Maturity brings us the ability to be concerned about ourselves and other people simultaneously and, consequently, to treat each in kind, considerate, compassionate, understanding, careful, and yet carefree, ways.

One attribute of maturity is the ability to delay gratification. Being aware that instant fulfillment, happiness, or resolution is a remote possibility at best is a sign of a mature outlook. Instant love among stepsiblings, instant compatibility between yourself and your stepkids, instant rapport between you and your husband regarding discipline and other kid stuff, instant anything, probably won't happen. The ability to delay gratification and wait for blessings to unfold is an invaluable asset when creating both a marriage and a stepfamily.

As a mature marriage partner, mother, and stepmom, we take ourselves and circumstances less seriously, are more confident about our abilities and talents, and more easily roll with the punches that inevitably come in families of all types. We have the patience to let relationships evolve in their own good time. In essence, maturing well means that we develop into an accepting and supportive friend to ourselves and, naturally, extend that understanding attitude toward those with whom we are in relationship.

Taking Responsibility

A very important aspect of maturity in marriage is the willingness to take responsibility for our own feelings and our own life. While it's true that we can bring out the best in each other, no one other than ourselves is in charge of our happiness. If we get caught in the trap of looking to our partner to provide our happiness and give us a sense of well-being, it stands to reason that our mate can also strip us of those same things.

Paradoxically, as an openhearted friend and partner, we want to bring happiness, health, and well-being to our mate, and we can do just that. However, we cannot *make* them happy, healthy, or wise. We can offer our unfailing support and unconditional love, but if they don't want to receive it, there's not a darn thing we can do about it. Each of us is responsible for our ability to both give and to receive love.

Pam and Chet, of whom I spoke earlier, combined her three children with his two. The kids were all thirteen and under, and Pam and Chet were thirty-four and thirty-three respectively when they married. She said, "We were mature and both very self-confident. I'd been widowed and single for many years. I didn't *need* a man. Both of us knew who we were and were just fine alone, and that made it much easier and more fun for us to be together." During their single years, they'd learned to take responsibility for their own "stuff." Chet and Pam married because they wanted to, not because they needed each other.

When Gene and I first came together, we were not quite the shining examples of taking personal responsibility that Pam and Chet were. I think we both idealized the other and in some secret crevice of our beings thought, "Ah, here is the person who will make me happy." We sustained those fantasies pretty well during

167

our courtship, but when we began to live together it was a different story. Add kids, stir, and—bye, bye fantasy.

During challenging times, we often lapsed into familiar but destructive habit patterns. Early on, Gene and I were excellent examples of masculine and feminine emotional stereotypes: I absorbed blame and took responsibility for making him happy, and he assigned blame and withdrew emotionally when he was unhappy. Neither absorbing nor assigning blame is grown-up behavior nor, as we discovered, was it very conducive to creating happiness or a sense of well-being for either of us. Acquiring the maturity and the wisdom to take responsibility for our own lives has, paradoxically, given us the freedom to intertwine our lives in more intimate and enjoyable ways.

I envision marriage as a temple with the marriage partners standing as the two entryway pillars. Each pillar is essential to the beauty and integrity of the whole structure and each also carries its share of the weight. Philosopher Kahlil Gibran, in his classic book *The Prophet*, encourages couples to "stand together yet not too near together: for the pillars of the temple stand apart. . . ." As we mature and learn to assume responsibility for our lives, we will be inviting, as Gibran put it, "the winds of heaven to dance between us."[1]

Complementary Interdependence

Gene came up with the term "complementary interdependence" to describe what we both wanted in our marriage. I love that concept. It epitomizes the reality that, although we continue to stand alone after marriage, we have also vowed to intimately link our life to the life of a chosen other. And marriage partners are intertwined by innumerable strands of energy that range from the wholly practical who-takes-out-the-trash variety to the sacred strands of sexual energy. When these connecting strands are complementary, equal, and fair, they enhance our lives immeasurably.

Complementary interdependence is an ever-evolving process of evolution, empowerment, and support in which partners share decision making as well as caretaking and caregiving. It reminds me of the miraculous workings of the physical body. Heart, brains, and bones do their own thing within the system and each part's function is vital to the survival of the whole. As good friends, marriage partners learn to recognize and respect each other's cycles of strength and vulnerability just as we learn to complement them with our own actions and attitudes.

Watching their parents and stepparents create a relationship rooted in friendship and complementary interdependence is extremely beneficial to all children but especially those whose nuclear family was unhappy. Our work toward and commitment to creating a grown-up marriage provides our children and stepchildren with a positive model for what marriage can be and, consequently, gives them both hope and tools for the success of their future love relationships.

Competition and Control Connote Power Struggles

Power struggles occur when complementary interdependence is abandoned. When we compete with each other or attempt to control our mate and/or the children we are usually vying for dominance. Unless we are psychologically astute and unfailingly mature, some power struggles seem to be a natural part of the developmental process of most relationships. Unfortunately, when children are involved power struggles can be magnified.

Taylor and Cal came to counseling because they were embroiled in a no-win power struggle concerning his nine-year-old daughter, Olivia. This was Taylor's first marriage and also her introduction to living with a child. Cal had custody of his daughter from his first marriage. "I do all of the physical care of this little girl," Taylor explained, "but have no decision-making or disciplinary power. I feel like they expect me to be a silent servant." Cal countered with, "But you're not Ollie's mother! You don't even know what a mother should be like."

To make matters worse, Olivia felt displaced as her father's main love and turned her anger on Taylor. In our discussions, Taylor acknowledged feeling jealous of Cal's daughter and Cal realized that he harbored a good deal of guilt about marrying and dividing his attention between Olivia and Taylor. His unwillingness to empower his wife in relationship to his daughter was an attempt to placate Olivia. In reality, seeing her father treat his wife disrespectfully was giving Olivia the idea that it was okay to disempower women, a belief that would not serve her well as a grown woman.

Because Taylor and Cal truly loved each other, were deeply committed to making their marriage work, and were each willing to take responsibility for their own part of the problem, this story has a happy ending. Olivia, now fifteen, is devoted to her four-year-old half-sister. Realizing how devastating competition, control, and poor communication can be, Cal and Taylor have worked diligently to improve their communication skills. They hightail it back to therapy whenever they hit a snag that they're unable to solve promptly by themselves. They now have a complementary partnership that enhances their lives and both their daughters' lives as well.

If we indulge in power struggles, it's probably because we want, or feel, that we need control in some area of our relationship. Self-righteousness, which is often linked with control issues, is a form of immaturity that keeps us stuck in power struggles. But since complementary partnership and control cannot coexist, it's important for us to quickly recognize a power struggle and back off. We need to gently but firmly examine our own motivations and feelings: Why do we need to win this confrontation or this particular point? What are we afraid of? Is this an old habit pattern reasserting itself? What old beliefs do we have that support our behavior? Are they valid now? Is the way we're acting constructive or destructive to our relationship?

Power struggles are dead ends on the road to both friendship and complementary interdependence. We need to turn from our power struggles and honestly explore the unique talents and attributes that each of us bring to our partnership. It doesn't matter what form our contribution takes. The one and only criterion for openhearted, grown-up, complementary interdependence is that each person feels like an equal and valuable partner.

MAKING TIME FOR LOVE AND PLAY

One of the main ways to strengthen our sacred bond with our mate is to make time for love and play. Finding time or energy (or privacy) for play and love can sometimes be difficult, but it is important that we don't let the difficulties become insurmountable. Love and play are too important to fall by the wayside.

A couple of the main reasons we married our husband is that we enjoy his company and are "hot to trot" to the bedroom. Adding children to the alchemy of our togetherness can provide some rather rude awakenings. I clearly remember the night when Gene and I, thinking all the children were asleep, eagerly met for a sexual date that we'd anticipated all day. We were jerked from the pleasure of the moment when one of my sons yelled down the hall, "Keep it quiet down there!" A very effective bucket of cold water, I can tell you. . . . But we didn't let that stop us. Love and play are too important in our sexual partnership.

Enjoying the Gift of Sexual Love

Sexual love is private love. While making love, we share a sacred and healing energy unique to the two of us and shared with no one else. Respectful, reverent, and spicy sex is the icing on our relationship cake, an openhearted and wonderful way to forge a passionate and fiery connection with our beloved. Sex is one of the original gifts from The Divine. Union with our beloved opens us to union with The Beloved.

Leslie ("The Rock") and Fred are very aware of the beautiful bonding possibilities of sexual love and wisely keep romance alive in their relationship. Very earnestly, Leslie told me, "I've never had a headache!" When Fred's three children lived with them, the children spent every other Sunday with their mother. "Those were our 'in-house' Sundays. And we've keep that luxurious tradition alive even now that the kids are out of the house," Leslie smiled. "We make love leisurely. We cook. We talk. We give each other undivided attention. It is simply *our* day." In the every-other-Sunday oasis they've created, Leslie and Fred enjoy the gift of sexual love and remember why they married each other in the first place.

Jeanne and Les are another great example of a couple committed to making time for themselves, even though they have five live-in children. Asked how they keep going in the midst of the daily demands of careers and kids, Jeanne answered, "Lots of lovemaking!" They budget to go away alone for one weekend every two months. "We allow ourselves two hours after we leave the house and one hour before going home to talk about the children," Jeanne said. "The rest of the time we talk about how *we* are. We catch up with each other and plug any leaks that may have sprung up the relationship."

In order to keep our relationships vital, alive, and charged with passionate energy, we need to make giving and receiving the gift of sexual love a priority. Doing so reconnects us to our partner and creates an ever strengthening bond between us physically, emotionally, and spiritually.

Step Lightly with Laughter and Play
Play is rehabilitating—that's why it's called re-creation. During play and laughter, our body produces healing and restorative chemicals called endorphins, which are natural tranquilizers. (And there were certainly many times during my active stepmothering career when I could have used some tranquilizing. How about you?) Laughter and play can be powerful connectors between us and our beloved as well as the children. Laughter helped Gene and me leap over many a hurdle, but fun was the first thing to go when we became ever-so-serious

about "stepping" or the game of life in general. Thankfully, we can now laugh about almost all of the times and trials we went through, and that is great. But how much better it would have been if we'd learned to take ourselves a little lighter a little earlier. We are still working on it.

Playing with our husbands is essential, for play catapults us into the childlike aspects of ourselves that are uncorrupted by circumstances, forever innocent, and naturally openhearted. The spontaneous and wonder-filled child in us is a good friend and an enthusiastic lover. She is also a lighthearted, loving mother and stepmother.

Encouraging the childlike part of ourselves to bring laughter and play into the bedroom brings an added bonus. Recently, Gene spent a good part of the day washing windows, while I was diligently plugging away at this book. As a much deserved treat, we indulged in a late afternoon lovemaking session, and at a very sensual and sexy moment, he looked at me earnestly and uttered, "I also do windows!".

May Sarton once wrote, "Each day, and the living of it, has to be a conscious creation in which discipline and order are relieved with some play and pure foolishness."[2] We're never too old to play and be foolish. In fact I was telling the kids the other day that the grandmother they see before them now is a lot younger than the mother and stepmother they had. It's taken me a long time to grow young, but the fact that I am actually doing so is cause for joy.

CELEBRATING THE BOND BEYOND

Whether they are conscious of it or not, I believe most marriage partners carry a strong soul bond and friendship into their union. Why else would we choose this one person among all the rest? When Gene and I saw five falling stars on the night we first met, we felt as if the heavens were rejoicing over our meeting. Although we spent only a few hours together and didn't plan to meet again, Gene repeatedly dreamed about me until we made a date to see each other about a month later.

Jeanne, whom I spoke of earlier, had a similar experience. Before she met her husband, Les, she dreamed about a man she'd never seen before. Several days later, she recognized him immediately when she and Les met at a charity fund-raiser. They felt as if they had known each other forever. Combining five kids and dealing with a troublesome former wife is not easy, but from their first meeting, Les and Jeanne believed, "there was an agreement in place to do this thing."

Such a bond is a mystery that cannot be explained. Our soul connection is a bond beyond the children given into our care and will continue after they leave our homes. It is our bond alone, a precious gift to be celebrated, cherished, and nurtured.

Kathy, whose stepmothering journey resembles The Perils of Pauline, offers this advice to other stepmothers: "Realize that the relationship with your partner is the most important thing. That's what you're going for in the long run. Focus on the relationship and make your man do the same. Also keep remembering how lucky the kids are to have you both." After seeing Kathy and her husband together, I feel her advice must be working for them. Amid bitter and backbiting behavior from the children and other family and friends, they are happy with each other. They bucked heavy odds to be together and, while life continues to be difficult, they are convinced that it is right to be sharing their lives with each other.

A plaque that Gene gave me hangs in our kitchen. It reads, "Happiness is being married to your best friend." How true. At its strongest and most fulfilling, marriage is an openhearted friendship between equals. Such a committed and mature union can bring out the best in us, guide us as we continually evolve and develop, and fill our hearts with the healing power of laughter and joy.

Communication Is The Heart of Marriage

If you ever expect to be loved,
you must reveal who you are.

—LEO BUSCAGLIA

Two of the most seductive aspects of falling in love are the delight we take in revealing ourselves to our beloved and our insatiable desire to know all about him. During courtship, most couples open their hearts to each other, talking endlessly about themselves, each other, their relationship, and everything else under the sun. Couples who continue this communication pattern usually thrive, because communication is the heart of marriage. The essence of our connection with each other flows from our communication, whether it comes through talking, touching, or making love. Even when we don't realize it, if we love each other and live together, we are always communicating both verbally and nonverbally. When the communication between us is trustworthy and loving, we become closer and more deeply connected with each other.

Unfortunately, all too often the effortless communication of courtship seems to dissipate with marriage. Lack of communication is a serious problem in many marriages. In fact, the main sadness and frustration voiced by the stepmothers I interviewed revolved around their inability to communicate honestly and easily with their husbands. When communication is defensive, dishonest, or closed, it becomes a black hole, sucking vitality from us and our relationship. Many connections are severed and chasms created when couples communicate poorly with each other and/or their children.

As a therapist, I offer three words of advice to couples: communicate, communicate, communicate. Of course, I am urging constructive, loving, and thoughtful communication, not that which destroys or devalues either person. Constructive communication invites couples to reveal themselves to each other, builds connections between them, and strengthens love, commitment, and understanding; destructive communication makes us feel unsafe and can easily tear down and destroy all that we value between us. Luckily, with desire and intention, constructive communication can be learned.

A FEW BASIC SKILLS

Much can be said and learned about communication. The few basic communication skills shared here are by no means an exhaustive exploration of the topic, but I hope you'll find some practical suggestions to help you and your loved ones enjoy clearer communication and a deeper relationship with each other. Some simple communication savvy can go a long way in helping create happy, healthy marriages and stepfamily relationships.

Goals of Constructive Communication: Understanding and Connection

The loving goal of constructive verbal communication is, that as a result of sharing, we come to a deeper understanding of and closer connection with each other. It's also nice when we can reach some sort of a mutual agreement, but there are times when we may simply need to agree to disagree. Winning is never the goal of constructive communication. If you find that your jaws are locked, your heels are dug in, and you know you're right, you can bet your bottom dollar that your goal is to win this particular encounter. When you notice those symptoms, take a deep breath, back off, and without judgment say something like, "I just became aware that I'm really invested in winning right now. I'd like to take a break in order to pry myself out of my righteous mode. I'll let you know when I've successfully done that, and we can set a time to continue talking."

Straightforwardly accepting responsibility for any attitudes that are detrimental to positive communication between you and your mate creates a wonderful base of safety and maturity upon which to build. Being able to say, in effect, "Whoops, I'm off center here. Let me regroup" is a tremendously grown-up and loving approach to establishing constructive communication patterns.

John Wesley, founder of the Methodist Church, asked his parishioners questions that I think also apply to disagreeing marriage partners, "Though we cannot think alike, may we not love alike? May we be of one heart, even though we are not of one opinion?" Being of one heart, having a deeper understanding of what makes our beloved tick, and creating a closer connection between the two of us far outshines the momentary pleasure of "winning" a conversational round.

Dumping Defenses

Along with giving up the need to win, we also need to dump our defenses. We human beings are easily wounded and, to protect ourselves, have learned well that the best offense is a good defense. But the "best offense" usually gives offense in intimate relationships.

When I first encountered the adage, "In my defenselessness, my safety lies"[1] in the Course in Miracles my instant response was "In your dreams!" As a Class-A Wimp at the time, I imagined it would be heavenly and empowering to act out my defensive feelings on occasion. But that darn statement kept circling my consciousness until I finally *got* it. It didn't matter that I wasn't acting defensive: I often *felt* defensive and that was what I needed to give up. But to genuinely give up my defenses, I needed to heal the fears that triggered them.

Defensiveness is vulnerability with fangs. When we feel defensive, it's a sure sign that we also feel fearful. Clearly realizing the connection between fear and defensiveness may be enough to help us dump defensive behavior. With that awareness, we can often move past our righteousness and ask ourselves what we are afraid of. Couples can help each other dump defensiveness by agreeing to gently tell each other when they notice defensiveness baring its fangs. In one couple I know, the husband is the one most adept at this awareness and he has defused many a defensive moment by asking his wife, with genuine interest and concern "What are you afraid of right now?"

Just because we feel defensive, we needn't act that way. Our feelings may impel us toward action but they don't compel us to act in destructive ways. As mature adults, we can honor our impulses and explore the feelings that cause them, and we can choose to act constructively.

Defensiveness brings out the anger within everyone involved and does nothing to further our understanding of ourselves or our beloved. Nor does it help us connect more deeply to each other. On the contrary, defenses effectively build up "da fences" between us. The Chinese proverb, "If you are patient in one moment of anger, you will escape a hundred days of sorrow" offers wise counsel. Dumping our defenses helps strengthen our marriage and allows us to become better friends with our mate.

Agreeing on a Time to Talk

One of the quickest ways to send you mate diving into a defensiveness bunker is to say, "We need to talk *now*!" In my younger days, when fear of rejection ruled and feeling disconnected from Gene ranked second only to being condemned to death, I often demanded instant communication. Oh, boy, was that a mistake! Without any forewarning or time to ponder how he felt or what he wanted to say concerning certain issues, Gene inevitably became defensive. Who could blame him? There have been a few times when he demanded instant communication, and I responded defensively too. When we're ambushed, it's natural to back up and bare our fangs. Though natural, desiring instant communication is not conducive to promoting understanding or close connections.

Over the years, Gene and I learned a simple but effective three-step technique that helps avert defensiveness:

1. We tell each other that we need to talk.
2. We outline what our issues or concerns are.
3. We ask our partner to pick a time within the next twenty-four hours when he/she is willing to talk.

Of course, if there is an immediate crisis, you may need to talk sooner, but you can still follow the steps and respect your mate by giving them the choice of when within the next half-hour or so they would be willing to get together.

For communication to be optimal, both parties need to believe that they have freely chosen to be present. That may not mean that either of us *wants* to be present, it simply means that we have made a mature and grown-up agreement to confront the issues and concerns on the table.

Unfinished Business is an Energy Leak

Unless we are extremely argumentative and/or volatile, no one really relishes confrontation, no matter how gentle it is. Most of us crave peace and harmony and would love to avoid talking about difficult and emotional issues. But unfinished business depletes our relationships as surely as a tiny pinprick eventually deflates a balloon.

"Neither Les nor I can manage unfinished business," Jeanne told me. "Our relationship comes first, and we have strong communication with each other, so there are times when we talk until 2:00 a.m. If the kids need us, they just have to wait. And if the issue concerns one of them, we wake them up when we come to an agreement."

Jeanne and Les live the philosophy that a couple should never go to bed angry. While immediately "talking it out" works for some couples, each couple will create the communication style and practice that works for them. In theory, I believe it's a good idea not to go to bed angry, but in practice I've done it many times because I often know something is amiss, long before I have a clear idea of what's bugging me. I do let Gene know that I'm exploring feelings that will need to be discussed later, but I ferret around and find my feelings either on my own or by talking with select women friends. Very often I will also pray, meditate, and write in my journal for clarification.

What works for Jeanne and Les or Gene and me may not work for you and your husband, but these are only a couple of the options. Because few of us are born with good communication skills, it may be extremely helpful for both of you to seek out the services of a therapist or enroll in a class in order to become more skillful communicators. Make a sincere commitment to find a style that suits you as a couple, for communication is the life-enhancing heart of your marriage. When you have good ways of communicating, unfinished business will never linger long enough to deflate your relationship.

THREE CRUCIAL KEYS —
LOVING, LISTENING, LEARNING

To start practicing the art of constructive communication, we need remember only these three crucial keys:

1. Come from LOVE and remain grounded in LOVE.
2. LISTEN deeply and attentively from your heart.
3. LEARN to understand your beloved, and teach him to understand and listen to you.

Loving

Constructive communication is always grounded in love. While we may not feel the least bit loving at the time, asking the simple question, "What is loving right now?" can help cool many a heated moment. If we can't respond positively and, at least metaphorically, open our hearts and arms to our mate, it's probably good to take a time out until our tempers cool a bit.

The late Leo Buscaglia, once the reigning prince of love and hugs said, "Nine times out of ten, when you extend your arms to someone, they will step in, because basically they need precisely what you need."[2] And what are these needs? To be loved, accepted, and understood are on top of almost everyone's list. Communicating lovingly—or at least with the *intention* toward loving—keeps the lines of communication clear and the heart ties secure.

Listening

Joyce, a dear stepmother friend of mine, is married to a man who can be rather difficult. Because of his wounding childhood, her husband is often a bear to communicate with, yet she has learned to do so effectively. "How do you do it?" I asked her. "Two ways," she answered. "First, I encourage him to keep talking about his miseries, angers, and resentments. (Of course, I had to get smart enough to detach and not "take the bait" he threw out.) He talks and talks and I keep clarifying and clarifying. I keep asking more questions and keep doing reality checks with him. But, mainly, I listen and clarify, listen and clarify."

Lest we all feel inadequate in the light of Joyce's wisdom and patience, I'll tell you a secret. She has two graduate degrees in psychology, has been a therapist for many years, and occasionally I answer the phone to hear her long, loud scream. "Hi, Joyce, what's he done now?" I ask. After she vents some frustration, we usually have a good laugh and then she tells me what she's learned to understand better about her husband by listening and clarifying this latest time.

I love the fact that LISTEN has the exact same letters as the word SILENT. Out of love, we need to be silent and listen in order to truly understand our man. And, of course, he needs to do the same for us.

Learning

Not listening closely leads us to make erroneous assumptions. Murphy's Bar & Grill in Boulder has a plaque on the wall that reads, "Assumption is the mother of all screwups." Both wise and true. Assuming we understand is an invitation to surprise, shock, and misunderstanding.

Only through listening and clarifying can couples hope to understand each other. Understanding ourselves is hard enough, so, in order to understand our mate, it's especially important that we listen with love and with the goal of learning to understand them more deeply and fully.

Only by learning to understand someone can we provide the emotional support and climate they need to thrive and grow. Without understanding what is important to someone we love, we may project onto them what is important to us and, thereby, not fill their needs at all. For instance, early in our relationship I assumed that Gene was as crazy about birthday celebrations as I was, and so I planned elaborate parties and festivities for him. Although appreciative, he really didn't care about celebrating in a big way. Over the years I've learned to make his birthday celebrations low-key and he's learned to honor the fact that I get a big charge out of high-key birthday bashes.

More intimately, through both heartful and hurtful communication, we've also learned to understand each other's vulnerabilities. Gene knows how vulnerable I am to anything that even hints of criticism, and I'm aware of how vulnerable he is when he thinks he's handled a situation imperfectly. Because we respect one another's soft, defenseless spots and try never to wound each other intentionally, we are careful to deal gently with sensitive issues. More often than not, we now succeed. But sometimes we don't. Ironically, in the long run, not succeeding often brings us even greater understanding of each other. Learning to understand each other helps insure that we will not inadvertently wound those we love but will, in fact, love them more wisely and beautifully.

Sex, money, kids, discipline, hurt feelings, competition, and, of course, "them exes" can all be thrown in the hopper labeled "Hard Stuff." In stepfamilies, laden as they are with complications and convoluted feelings, it's especially important to share the hard stuff, but it's also important to do it gently, compassionately, and diplomatically.

Gently, Gently, Gently

Considering the fact that we're all laced with flaws, idiosyncrasies, and vulnerabilities, wouldn't it be wise and kind to adopt an attitude of gentleness in relating to each other? Wise, kind, *and* practical. Approached with gentleness and kindness, we are less likely to lash out, ignore, or react in a destructive manner.

"Don't just *do* something, *stand* there!" I love this wonderful twist to the old maxim because it's such valuable advice for communication. When we're quick to act and react, we're liable to *attack,* which is detrimental to any family encounter. Stand there, wait, ponder. Breathe. Let things inside simmer down. Collect your thoughts, sort out your feelings, and calm yourself. While waiting until the time is right to communicate an idea or feeling, I often visualize the waters of a pond slowly stilling after a rock has been thrown in. Pausing gives us the opportunity to arrive at an internal place from which we can choose wisely what needs to be done or said, and then do so gently.

Sharing the Hard Stuff the Easy Way: "I" Messages

There is one communication technique that stands head and shoulders above the rest. It forestalls blame and judgment, defuses defensiveness, and creates a loving atmosphere in which we can open our hearts and souls to each other. Called an "I" message, it's very simple to learn but not easy to remember when feelings are running high. "I" messages assist us in telling the truth without blaming or being hurtful. They are especially helpful when dealing with sensitive subjects, such as each other's children.

The formula for an "I" message is: "When you do or say (_____), I feel (_____)." The first part of the formula is factual: when you slam the door, when you turn away, or whatever. The second part expresses the feelings you feel in response to the words said or actions done. The idea is to express real feelings or a word picture that represents a real feeling, and not judgments or accusations. Use one or two words to describe a real feeling, such as confused, angry, abandoned, hurt, exhausted, discouraged, uncomfortable, joyful, or excited. Feelings describe what's happening to you, rather than a judgment about whatever the other person is doing. Here are two examples of clear "I" messages: "When you turn away from me when I'm talking, I feel rejected and angry," or "When you support me in a confrontation with the kids, I feel loved and sexually drawn to you." As you can see by the examples, "I" messages are not limited to expressing difficult emotions. They are equally good for dispensing appreciation and praise.

"You" messages, by contrast, make judgments, criticize, assume, and demean. The difficult "I" message above could easily have been sent as a "you" message: "When you turn away from me when I'm talking, you're being rude and inconsiderate," or, "You make me feel awful when you turn away. You hurt me!" The silent tag line at the end of a "you" message is, "You bastard, you!" "You" messages assume that the other person is responsible for our feelings. They're not. Only we are responsible for how we feel. It is our responsibility to share our feelings, honestly, gently, and nonjudgmentally.

"I" messages *inform*. "You" messages *attack*.

Examples:

"You" messages	*"I" messages*
You love your kids more than you do me.	Sometimes when you pay so much attention to your kids, I feel left out, like a grade school kid not chosen for a team on the playground.

| Your kids are disrespectful slobs. | When the kids leave all their messes for me to clean up, I feel like a slave who gets no respect. |
| If you cared about our marriage, you'd talk to me. | When you don't talk about how about you feel, I get lonely and afraid we won't make it. |

These examples highlight the difference in tone and intent between "I" messages and "you" messages. Which would you rather hear?

The "I" message is an extremely simple but important communications tool—and it's totally portable. You can use the "I" messages anywhere—at home, at work, even with yourself! Using "I" messages regularly will take practice, but using them well will greatly increase your ability to communicate clearly, effectively, and gently.

Essentially, It's You 'n' Me

When we can share the hard stuff gently, compassionately, and without judgment, we deepen our friendship with our husband and the kids through loving respect and mutual understanding. Our connection and friendship with our partner and paramour is paramount. Of course, we need to talk about the kids and focus some attention on them, but our couplehood deserves to be our priority and primary focus.

Thankfully, the longer we are together and the better we know each other, the more we grow to understand how to communicate and relate with a minimum of defensiveness, blaming, and misunderstanding. Many benefits are to be reaped by making the commitment to love, listen, learn, and gently be present to each other as dear friends and lovers. It's essential for us to remember that the core of our family, now and after the kids are grown, is "you 'n' me, baby."

PART FIVE

Embracing The Kids

It's so clear that you have to cherish everyone.
I think that's what I get from these older black women,
that sense that every soul is to be cherished,
that every flower is to bloom.

—ALICE WALKER

Embracing children other than your own may be the easiest thing you've ever done, or it may be the hardest. But, here they are, in your life. While we may consider the association with our stepchildren one based solely on chance and circumstance, what if that isn't true? What if individual souls gravitate together for a chance to facilitate each other's blooming? What if, in those wonderful cases of love at first hug, our meeting with a particular stepchild is simply a joyous connection with a kindred soul?

Wouldn't it be easier to cherish our stepchildren if we believed there was purpose and potential in our being together rather than assuming we were foisted on each other by mere chance? Adopting such a philosophy— you may be more comfortable calling it a fantasy, and that's perfectly okay—can make us feel like a willing participant in an opportunity for soul growth rather than a hapless victim of circumstance.

Although we are rarely consciously aware of it, I believe that relationships may be orchestrated by our souls for own evolution and unfoldment. Each of us has experienced meeting individuals whom we seem to intuitively recognize and then others who we instinctively want to stay away from.

While the concept of soul recognition resonates with my heart, it might not with yours. In actuality, it doesn't matter why or how certain people walk over the thresholds of our lives. If they are there, we are called to cherish them, as Alice Walker learned. Both our own children and our stepchildren will bring us joy and sorrow. Quite possibly, by stretching us beyond our preconceived limits of strength and patience, they will also become our finest teachers. They have the capacity to awaken within us greater courage and wisdom than we dreamed we possessed.

The vast majority of stepmothers I know sincerely desire to take their husband's children into their hearts. But wanting to embrace his children and being able to are sometimes two different things even with the most loving women. I've found that most of us fall somewhere between loathing and immediately loving our stepkids, especially during the first discombobulating years when everyone is attempting to adjust to the new familial arrangements.

Even if we fall head over heels in love with our stepkids at first sight, there will be times when the only embrace we can imagine giving them will be a hammer-lock. Not to worry. Our job description does not include *feeling* loving every moment of every day. During difficult times we can choose to embrace the kids either energetically or from a distance, rather than up close and personal. Or we can turn them over to divine helpers. While that may sound esoteric, it's actually easy to do. Simply picture the children, or child, in your mind's eye and send loving energy to them from your heart. If that's more than you can manage, ask their guardian angels to surround them with love and protection. Sometimes I find it very comforting to gently place a child or stepchild in the loving embrace of God, especially if I'm unable to emotionally or physically embrace them myself. No matter how we choose to send love, please remember that our *intention* to be loving is much more important than any technique.

Whether we believe our relationships are accidental or orchestrated by compassionate though unseen hands, the challenge to cherish remains the same. At our core, we are loving and spiritual beings. And as such, we are invited to embrace everyone who comes into our life. Sometimes love will flow effortlessly from a wellspring within us and, at other times, we'll simply wish everyone would go away and leave us alone. It doesn't matter. As long as our intention is to live from our hearts—embracing and cherishing each person, including ourselves—we will be doing the soul work we were meant to do.

The Heart of the Matter

*Men must take care of women, and women must
take care of men, and we must all take
care of the children. This must be our voice
in everything we do and everywhere we go.
It's not just a Hallmark card,
to talk about love being the answer.*

—MARIANNE WILLIAMSON

Today I had an experience that touched my heart in a universal woman/child way. I was in the backyard watering flowers and saw my next-door neighbor and her three-year-old daughter in their yard, also watering. The mom and I exchanged greetings and then I bent down and said, "Hello, Kelly Rosie!" to the little girl. Usually shy, Kelly surprised me by flinging up her little arms and running pell-mell into mine. While I held her and talked with her mom, Kelly Rose kept her sweet blond head snuggled into the curve of my neck. My heart was just as warmed, opened, and blessed as it would have been if this child were mine.

However, love is not always a feeling; it's something we participate in. With each little decision we make, we can choose to act in loving ways and be kind, caring, and compassionate to those children given into our care, if only for one weekend a month or a few visits in the summer. Let me reiterate that the love I'm talking about does not require that we *like* all the kids all the time—or even feel personally attracted to them. It simply means that we are willing to open our hearts and create a climate of love and caring that can allow a natural bond to emerge, if possible. If one never does, that's okay too, as long as our actions are consistently kind.

As naturally relational beings, women, mothers, and stepmothers carry the light of love to their family members. Not only are we usually the heart of the family, but we also act as the hearths around which the family gathers to warm itself. That may sound like too much responsibility, but, in reality, the best thing we can do to be both heart and hearth for our combined family is to relax.

Relaxing and realizing that everything—even the most difficult challenges—is temporary makes it easier to act from our hearts, to open ourselves, and to embrace the natural and appropriate bonds that can form between ourselves and our stepkids.

ADOPTING AN ATTITUDE OF HOSPITALITY

I once heard a sermon in which the Rev. Jean Scott encouraged listeners to adopt an attitude of hospitality rather than hostility, explaining that hospitality was an attitude of the heart. Bingo, I thought. That's what often happens in stepfamilies. Some of us get caught in the grip of hostility rather than hospitality toward each other. Feeling hostile means that we've fallen from our hearts and are being governed by the fear that reigns in our guts.

To be fair, I believe that most stepmothers initially greet their husband's children with open hearts. But, if we're rebuffed by a child's hostility, it takes a lot of determination and commitment not to respond in kind. Pam, whom we met earlier, said, "One of the hardest things for me was the fact that I didn't like one of my husband's kids. I thought I'd always like all kids, but this boy was mean and nasty." Luckily Pam is also psychologically savvy. "I knew enough psychology to understand that it was the rejection he felt from his own mother that caused his mean-spiritedness. Out of that awareness, I just chose to act compassionately," she said. "I did active listening, set limits, and was there for him as much as possible. But it was still hard. I wanted to really like him but never could."

Pam did what all of us are capable of doing. She acknowledged her difficult feelings and chose to adopt an attitude of hospitality anyway. Not that she let her stepson be mean and nasty to everyone, she didn't. But, totally on purpose, she welcomed him and did what she could for him. Eventually she was also able to forgive herself for not being able to like him.

Feelings may not always be subject to change, but attitudes are. As a result of making conscious commitments to adopt open-hearted attitudes, however, sometimes our feelings *do* change. When that happens, it's grace at work. Equally gratifying as the softening our own emotions is the sunny feeling we get when a stepchild's hostility melts in the warmth of our continued hospitality. I know that wonderful sense of grace from my own experience. For many years, I sincerely doubted that my stepdaughter and I would ever make peace, let alone feel close to each other, but we did and do—a turn of events for which I'm extremely grateful.

Letting Children (and Dogs) Teach Us

Benedictine Br. David Steindl-Rast tells his students, "Most of our day is gift after gift, if we wake up to it."[1] The same can be true for stepmothering when we expect and accept the lessons inherent in a merged family and wake up to the gifts presented to us each day. Now, I'm fully aware that some gifts have very prickly wrappings. These are gifts that can catapult us into the necessity of dealing with our carefully hidden stuff and growing our souls in the process.

One "gift" that darkened many of my days and brought me face to face with an aspect of my shadow, came in the form of a yippy little Austrian Silky dog named Nikki. Nikki had been the family pet in Gene's other family. However, when we moved from Hawaii, I was informed that Nikki would be sent to the animal shelter if we didn't take him to California with us. To complicate matters, on the one or two occasions when I'd seen Nikki, it had been hate at first sight for both of us, and Gene and I already had two big dogs of our own.

What a bind. If I said "no" to taking the dog, I would be the wicked stepmother personified and Nikki would, presumably, be a goner. If I said "yes," I'd be ticked off to the max. But, as you probably guessed, the damn dog came with us.

For childhood reasons that don't need to be explored here, one of my shadow aspects is jealousy, or the "green-eyed monster," as my mother called it. Having Nikki with us brought every one of those green-eyed monsters raging to the fore. I hated the fact that Nikki represented Gene's former life and felt jealous when the dog took up permanent residence on Gene's lap. It was especially galling to watch Gene stroke "that dog" when he had emotionally withdrawn from me into some unreachable realm. I already felt competition from one of his daughters for Gene's affection and attention. Now I had more competition from a skinny little dog that I didn't like, was pressured to take, and definitely didn't want. Yuck!

I really had little choice but to meet each green-eyed monster head-on, wrestle it to the floor, and transform its energy through therapy and much self-examination. And Nikki barked and basked in Gene's affection through it all. In retrospect, I'm thankful for that dog's assistance and thrilled he helped free me from most of the jealousy that I'd fought with all my life. But I also know that if there is an actual hell, and I am unfortunate enough to go there, that dog, yipping wildly, will greet me at the burning gates.

While they may not come covered in fur, many gifts and lessons will await you in the stepmothering domain. Naturally, the kids themselves are the biggest gifts and usually provide the most education. But there will be others that come with the kids that, more than likely, will introduce you to parts of your shadow side. Take it from one who knows—you're better off being hospitable to these "gifts" and learning what you can from them, because they're probably going to hang around until you learn the lessons they offer.

By their very nature, children have much to teach us. When we can open our arms, hearts, and minds to their instruction, we'll be amazed how much we can gain from being in relationship with them. For example, children often act as great models of acceptance and hospitality by embracing each other as siblings long before we adults are able to conceive of everyone as part of a cohesive whole. In our family, my boys were intrigued to have little sisters and the girls relished the adventure that the boys brought to their lives. Because of the age and gender differences, they avoided the kind of competition traps that can absolutely annihilate stepfamily peace and togetherness.

In some cases, stepmothers reported that the sibling rivalry between stepbrothers and stepsisters continued into adulthood, but for the most part the children accepted each other quickly. My son Brett, when asked what he would suggest to stepfamilies, responded thoughtfully, "Let's see, I don't know. What I *do* know is that I consider Lynnie and Paige my *real* sisters, and you guys [meaning Gene and myself] helped that happen." Although Brett couldn't pinpoint how he thought we'd helped, I believe the two most useful things were that the kids spent so much time together and that we tried our darnest to be fair in our dealings with each of them.

Watching our kids extend hospitality to each other and "blend" with each other relatively seamlessly gave me hope that the whole family might eventually follow their lead. It didn't happen overnight. In fact, it would be closer to the truth to say that it happened just a few years ago, but, as of now, we are close and definitely consider ourselves "a family."

Because your situation is different than mine or anyone else's, your kids may not greet each other with open arms. Some rivalry is natural, but if the children don't like each other or fight an abnormal amount, perhaps you're being asked to learn the lesson of speaking up more quickly, as stepmom Kathy wishes she had. "My husband's two youngest kids were, and still are, mean to my daughter and they exclude her. It hurts me so much to see her hurt," Kathy said. "I wish I'd put my foot down earlier concerning their being mean to April and disrespectful to adults."

When the children are acting out against their siblings or parent figures, ask yourself what lessons there are for you to learn about your own behavior as well as theirs in any given incident. If you remain mystified and the situation doesn't solve itself fairly quickly, it's a good idea to seek some help outside the stepfamily circle.

Even though the amount of dirt spread and food consumed increases in direct proportion to the number of feet and mouths in your home, so, thankfully, do the possibilities for laughter and love increase as well. Adopting an attitude of hospitality toward all of the people in your family-by-marriage helps you embrace the challenges, lessons, and love inherent to your stepmothering role. But, it's so important to bear in mind that it all takes time.

Hang in There

I wish I had a dollar for every time a stepmother answered "Hang in there!" to the question, "What advice do you have for other stepmothers?" I could buy my own Caribbean island.

Stepmoms reported reaping their fair share of rewards and even accolades after the passage of years and the presence of much patience. Often indirectly, we may hear one of our stepchildren use a favorite phrase of ours, or see that they've adopted a value learned from us. In the best of all possible worlds, the love that we worked hard to give them returns to us in both tangible and intangible ways.

Angela, who had a rough time with her husband's four daughters, told me she "just plain hung in there." None of the girls embraced or accepted Angela when they were young. In fact, they never used her name and insisted on introducing her as "my father's wife." However, Angela recently received a Mother's Day card from one of her now-adult stepdaughters with a bluebird—which is Angela's symbol for happiness—and a handwritten note: "You are a role model for loving." With tears in her eyes, Angela said, "It's all worth it, every iota of pain and work."

One of the hardest challenges we can face is the difficulty our husbands and children may have accepting each other. It's best not to interfere, but because many of us are natural "fixers," we long to rush in and make everything copacetic between those we love. However, I learned from talking with stepchildren that it's best if we back off and give our men and children the opportunity to build their own hang-in-there muscles and forge their own relationships.

The rewards to be gleaned from other members of the family learning the fine art of hanging in there are many. For instance, Kayla, an adult stepdaughter, complimented her stepfather, "You know, I've got to hand it to my stepfather. He just hung in there and waited me out. From the very first, he treated me like his own daughter, even though I wouldn't have much to do with him. Now, as an adult, I really appreciate him and the effort that must have taken." My son Mike said, "In retrospect, what impresses me is that Gene just hung in there until he won me over."

Both Kayla and Mike admitted that their mothers—unfortunately that would be me, in Mike's case—actually hampered the adjustment process by being overly concerned and often interfering in confrontations between themselves and their stepfathers. Feedback gleaned from stepkids emphasized that things work much better when mothers can hang in there and let things be rather than butting in and trying to make things better.

I'm sure it would have helped me open my heart in those early years if I'd been able to talk to veteran stepmothers and been reassured that hanging it there eventually produced many blessings and brought much soul growth—that, in fact, it was all worth it. Talking with them would have helped me realize there was a light at the end of the tunnel. To a woman, stepmothers of adult children admitted that a huge bonus for "hanging in there" is the fact that eventually all of the children are on their own and we have our husbands mostly to ourselves. Maybe it would help us embrace an attitude of hospitality toward our stepchildren and better weather the myriad challenges inherent in the stepfamily process if we took their assurances and adopted their advice of "hang in there!" as our motto and rallying cry.

MOTHERING OUR OWN CHILDREN

Each day of our lives we're faced with choices, some monumental but most minuscule. When our choices impact the lives of our biological or adopted children, our primary responsibility is to mother the children we agreed to bring into our hearts and homes. This can get very sticky in stepfamilies because of the paradox that as women, wives, and mothers, we have three *first* choices, three *primary* responsibilities: ourselves, our mate, and our children.

I wish I'd handled this paradox differently in our combined family. As it was, I expected too much from my sons, Mike and Brett. Fearing that I might lose Gene, I expected my boys to be more flexible and understanding than I did him. If Gene became upset or angry, I relied heavily on my children to "make things right." In retrospect, it makes me cringe, but understanding the young woman I was then, I have come to forgive her.

Having been a single mom for four years before Gene and I got together, I was very close to my sons and implicitly trusted the bonds between us. Unfortunately, residual vulnerability from my first husband's jarring departure sloshed over into my relationship with Gene. My trust in his love for me—or probably more accurately, my own lovability—was more shallow than my trust in my boy's love. The result of that imbalance was that I relied on my kids to be more grown-up than they should have been at the time.

As a result of this and other factors, my oldest son, Mike, felt I'd abandoned him in our early stepfamily years. Mike adopted an adversarial stance with Gene from the start. I felt torn between the two of them and probably did choose Gene more often than I did Mike. As we were discussing this recently, Mike said, "But, you know, Mom, even if you'd been perfect, the situation was hell." For Mike, it was hell. He remembers sitting on the beach one day thinking, "Nobody loves me, and I didn't even get to bring my dog." (Hawaii quarantined incoming dogs for three to six months, and we all agreed it would be cruel to put Laddie through that. While we all missed him, Mike felt his loss most acutely.) Brett maintains that combining families was relatively easy for him. However, although it sounded like it would be wonderful, the culture shock of moving to Hawaii was hard for both boys.

As a result of my fear and emotional dependence, I'm sure I sold all four of us short in many ways. But given my immaturity, lack of wisdom, and wounds, I'm convinced that I did the best I could, and that's the reality upon which I base my self-forgiveness. Nonetheless, tears trickle down my face as I write this more than twenty years later.

That's another reality about stepfamilying: there always seem to be a few maverick tears hiding out in the emotional underbrush. At least that's true of the stepmothers I've talked with throughout the years. Many times we shared current and residual tears, especially about our own children's past and present pain.

What Our Kids Want and Need

There are many things that biological and adopted children want and need from their mothers. Let's take a quick look at some of the most important.

Attention and affection

First and foremost, our kids deserve to have a mother they can count on, one who gives them the attention and affection they need. To the best of her ability, kids need the *same* mother they had before the advent of the stepfamily. A few children I spoke with were saddened when their mothers metamorphosed primarily into Mrs. So and So after remarriage.

One such story came from Kayla, the young woman who complimented her stepfather earlier. When she was twelve, Kayla went to camp for the summer. As her mother drove her home after camp ended, she told Kayla that her best friend had moved away while Kayla was at camp. A little later in the car ride, Mom dropped another emotional bomb, informing Kayla that she was about to marry a man whom Kayla had never met.

When the poor hapless soon-to-be-stepfather opened the door to meet Kayla for the first time, he inadvertently let her dog out, and it was never seen again. If it hadn't been so painful, Kayla's saga was beginning to resemble a *Saturday Night Live* sketch. To make matters worse, a few months after her mom and new stepdad were married, they sent Kayla's only sibling, a brother, to boarding school after he was caught smoking marijuana. As the icing on the cake, Kayla's mom was so enthralled by her new husband that she, unwittingly and without malice, virtually ignored her daughter.

Within months Kayla lost her best friend, her dog, her mother, and her brother. Is it any wonder she felt bereft and abandoned?

To her credit, and to her mom's as well, Kayla said, "I never doubted that Mother loved me, and I was glad she was happy. I just missed her and didn't get the attention I wanted. I just wanted my mommy." I met Kayla at a wedding and was immediately drawn to her. She seemed like a genuinely sweet young woman and a very present and dedicated mother to her three-year-old daughter, Terren. So, who knows? Although her past was painful, maybe she's a better person because of it. I was thankful to hear that she and her mother have talked extensively about their past and are now enjoying a renewed relationship.

It boils down to this: No matter how many demands are made upon us, our kids want, need, and deserve enough UDA—undivided attention—to thrive. Sometimes as few as five minutes of absolute attention and/or affection at a time will fill that yawning need.

Security and continuity

Underscoring the need for security and continuity my son, Brett, said, "If we'd stayed in San Jose when you and Gene got married, and I'd gone to the same school and been able to see Dad on weekends, I think the whole stepfamily thing would have been no big deal for me."

As much as possible, our children need to have the grounding that familiar surroundings, routines, and people provide, especially when their actual family structure is being altered through our remarriage. Of course, that's not always possible, as it wasn't for Mike, Brett, and me.

To have you in their corner

All kids want their parents to go to bat for them, stand up for them, and champion their causes. This doesn't mean that we blindly say, "But, my boy would *never* do thus and so . . ." It does mean that our children need to know they can count on us to be there, listen to their side of each story, and unfailingly support them when they need it.

"Because I worked for myself," explained Suzanne, "I had the luxury of being home when the kids got home from school. Unobtrusively, I made myself available in case any of them had a need to talk. We sat in the kitchen while they snacked, and I listened about their day, the complaining and the excitement." She went on to explain, "My own mom was a housewife and she was always ready to listen when I got home from school, and I *always* talked." Suzanne told me that her mother's availability had been extremely important to her and she wanted to provide the same nurturing and support for her kids and stepkids.

I, like Suzanne, could always count on my mother to listen to me and go to bat for me in situations that seemed unfair or disturbing. Being sure of my mother's unfailing interest and support was probably my main security as a youngster.

A neutral—or better—working relationship between you and their father

Nothing tears kids apart like having their parents at each other's throats. All the stepkids and kids from divorced families stressed one thing: The hardest thing is when their real parents don't get along and/or bad-mouth each other. Equally emphatically they said, Never, never should a stepparent say anything negative about their stepchild's natural mom or dad.

While I think most stepmoms are sensitive enough not to speak in uncomplimentary ways about a stepchild's real parent, the same is not always true concerning your children's other parent. Having parents disparage each other is very painful for children and makes them extremely uncomfortable. For the kids' sake, we need to be mature in our dealings with our former mates and keep our encounters with them as calm as possible. Getting along with their father is truly a wonderful gift that we can give our children.

Flexibility and generosity regarding visits, holidays, and other family gatherings

Ah, yes, the holiday trauma . . . I know it well. Holidays carry a lot of emotional energy for most of us. Because of the feelings embedded in special occasions, we need to be our most mature, flexible, and generous selves regarding what the kids want to do and what is best for everyone concerned.

Hopefully, by the time you read this, you've figured out the logistics of holidays, visits, and family gatherings and, with any luck, have moved through the more searing emotional trauma of not being with your children on special occasions. You also have a mate now with whom you can share holidays, which makes them immeasurably better. (I don't know about you, but some of my single, sans-kids holidays were among the saddest times I've had in my life.)

Sometimes more difficult than seeing the kids off to their dad's house are the occasions, such as graduations, weddings, funerals, grandbaby births or birthdays, when all the parents and stepparents need to be together. If there is hostility and animosity between parents at these affairs, the children's joy is dimmed and they suffer inordinately. No matter how uncomfortable we may feel around former spouses, for the children's sake we need to call up our most mature selves, put aside our own feelings while together, and think only of the kids and what they need from us right now. It's simply a matter of making the loving choice.

Freedom to work out their own relationship with their stepfather

I admitted earlier, I failed pretty miserably in this area. If I were to do it over, I'd essentially *butt out*, hang in there, and trust Gene, Brett, and Mike to forge their own bonds—or not. As Mike eventually let me know, nothing I did made them any closer. If I'd had the wisdom to graciously step aside from the start, trusting the three of them to create their own relationships in their own time, I could have saved us all a lot of grief.

Unconditional love and support

Any children that we bring into the world or invite into our lives through adoption deserve our unconditional love and support. At the beginning of our children's lives, we are their universe. To a great extent, in relationship to us, they form their relationship to themselves and to the world. By observing our actions and attitudes toward them, they determine whether or not their needs are important and begin to acquire belief systems about their inherent worth and lovability.

As our kids grow, the circle of influence around them expands. The stronger and more stable our relationship, the farther and stronger they are able soar in their personal lives, especially when they know they are held in our hearts at all times. Unconditionally loved and supported by us, more than likely our children will be able to give that same quality of love to themselves and those with whom they relate. Truly, unconditional love and support is the wind beneath our children's wings. They deserve nothing less.

BEFRIENDING OUR STEPCHILDREN

We may grow to unconditionally love and support our stepchildren as well as our own, but a more realistic goal—at least for the first few years—is simply to befriend our stepkids. Love is such a loaded word in our culture that we set ourselves up to feel like failures if we use it willy-nilly in our stepfamilies. It's more gently realistic to substitute the idea of being caring and kind to our stepchildren rather than telling ourselves that we love them immediately. We can choose to befriend our stepkids and to act in loving ways, but experiencing the feelings of love itself is a mystery that's not ours to command or control.

Heather, a stepmother of two girls who visited on holidays and in the summer said, "On the whole it was just pleasant and nice to have the kids." As a mother herself, she added, "There is a difference in the way you feel about your own kids. There is a tiny space that remains open and objective with your stepchildren." That tiny, open, objective space can help us relate to our stepchildren directly from our hearts. With a smidgen of compassionate detachment, we can more easily discern what is needed in the moment.

We can befriend the kids by providing consistent safety and caring when they are with us—and trusting all will be well when they're not with us. While there are scores of ways to care for kids and provide a safe home for them, I want to illustrate just a few here.

Honor Feelings

To create a climate of caring and emotional safety in our homes, each person's feelings need to be honored. I vividly remember one twilight hour when my sixteen-year-old stepdaughter, Lynnie, erupted into the house sobbing wildly. The four of us who were home surrounded and held her until she was calm enough to gasp out what was wrong. The cause of her upset was that she'd hit a cat on the drive home, so we all piled in the car to search for the injured animal. Although we never found the kitty—which we all agreed must mean it wasn't seriously hurt—we did provide a safe place for

Lynnie to express her sadness and we continued to console her until she felt better and calmer.

Feelings are rampant little beasties in kids, and it can take quite a lot of patience and commitment not to negate children's emotions by saying something like, "Oh, for heaven's sake, that's not important!" or "That's silly. Why would you feel that way?" Especially if we feel targeted by a stepchild's feelings, it's easy to respond out of hurt, impatience, or ignorance—but we must learn not to. Part of the stepmom's challenge is finding creative, caring, supportive ways of responding to the kids' emotional turmoil without discounting, invalidating, or minimizing their feelings.

Meredith, a stepmother to one little girl, told me, "It took some hefty teeth-clenching to keep from reacting when my six-year-old stepdaughter yelled at me, counting the ways in which I wasn't as good as her mommy. Thankfully, I was able to talk to my sister who had been a stepmother for fourteen years. She helped me come up with some responses to use when Gillian spewed venom at me. I actually wrote myself a list so I could refer to it when my own feelings were about to boil."

Here are some of the statements that Meredith and her sister came up with: "I can see you are really upset right now. Can you help me understand what it's about?"; "You are really feeling lousy right now, aren't you? What would help you feel better, do you think?";

and "Let's go out and throw some rocks in the pond and pretend we're throwing away our hard feelings, because I have some too right now." Though the statements are helpful, Meredith also sets limits. When she has had enough she tells Gillian, "I can listen for one more minute, and then I need to take a time-out. We can talk more later." She then sets the timer on the microwave and leaves the room when it rings.

"Things are getting better," Meredith said. "Gillian is getting progressively less angry, and I am a lot more patient!" With a very maternal smile, she continued, "She actually comes to me sometimes and says she misses her mommy and needs to be held. At first I didn't know if I could hold her after all the hurtful things she'd said, but then I remembered she's a kid and cut her some slack. I look forward to holding her now."

It sounds like Gillian is learning to sort through her feelings and not rely solely on expressing anger as a means of getting attention, support, and guidance. If her original feelings of anger had been squashed, she probably would not have been able to get past them to the softer and more central ones that her anger masked. Children deserve to have their feelings honored and need to be taught how to express them constructively. For children to learn to trust their own emotions, instincts, and intuition, it is vital to have caretakers who acknowledge and honor their feelings.

Welcome Visiting Kids

Especially when stepchildren visit irregularly, we need to find ways to welcome them, to make them feel as if they belong and have a place in our home. It's great if kids can have a room of their own, but when that's impossible, we can find spaces—such as drawers and closets—that they can call their own during their stays.

Like Gillian, visiting kids are likely to feel some homesickness and may act needy, rebellious, or sullen as a result. While grumpy, sad, or angry kids can set our teeth on edge, it's best to relax and wait out the transition time, to listen with an open heart balanced by firm limits, and to offer little emotional welcomes along the way. Sometimes it really helps smooth the adjustment period at the start of a visit when kids have time alone with their dad and don't need to relate to us or our children for a while.

Foster Closeness Between All Siblings

In order to foster closeness among all siblings, we need to be very careful when talking about each child. If you have issues with any child, it's better to talk them out with anyone but another child. Your own children are likely to feel protective of you. If they perceive a stepsibling hurting you, discussing it with them can taint their feelings toward the other child.

Another essential is trying to be as fair as possible with all of the children. Over and over stepmothers stressed the theme of fairness. "We were deeply committed to being fair with all the kids," said one mom. Another stated, "I'm sad to say that those kids who acted out got the most attention, but we really tried to treat each one equally." Kids are alarmingly perceptive. If they feel that they, or any child in the family, is receiving preferential treatment, a variety of feelings can surface. The favored one may rub it in, causing the other kids to feel less important than their siblings and ticked off or hurt as a result, or they may feel guilty and uncomfortable with the special treatment. Whatever the resultant feelings, an intention toward fairness is paramount for a combined family to function as a complementary unit.

There will probably be times when we need to act as mediator between sibs and stepsibs, or even between the kids and our husband and/or ourselves. Mediations require us to muster all the maturity we can find within ourselves. And it is especially hard for us to be a good and loving stepmom or wife if we think our kids are getting the shaft. When that's the case, it's best to find an impartial person to be the mediator. Feeling protective makes it almost impossible to be objective.

Along with being fair and acting as mediator, probably the most powerful thing we, as moms and stepmoms, can do to foster sibling closeness is to genuinely enjoy and value each child for their individual qualities, attributes, and foibles. We need to remember each child is a gift, even when he or she is also a challenge.

No Attempts to Mold into Your Own Image

Lana, mother of five and stepmother to one, confessed, "My kids' problems look like me. I didn't understand my stepson's problems. They looked like *his* mother and were foreign to me." Asked how she handled that, she answered, "Well, at first I tried to make him more like me, to integrate him into our family community, and instill values in him that I thought were important." But, she shared, that didn't work at all. In fact, her main regrets are that she didn't trust his dad more to make all the decisions regarding his own son and that she hadn't chosen more objectively to "be his friend, encourager, and supporter."

It's tempting to try and mold our stepkids into our own image so that we'll know how to relate to them more easily. But it doesn't work for stepkids any better than it does for our own kids. It's best to simply let that idea go.

Compassionate Detachment

Although we usually prefer personal, warm-fuzzy love in our family circles, sometimes the ability to detach compassionately is as good as it gets *and* we can congratulate ourselves mightily when we're able to do *it*!

In actuality, finding freedom and peace of mind in many situations often lies in acceptance of the situation. I found detached acceptance my only option with my stepdaughter Paige. Outside of setting limits or moving out, there was little I could do about the fact that she was, in her words, "testing Dad to see if he would choose his wife or his daughter."

After much breast beating and self-pity, I tried to view the situation as an opportunity for spiritual growth and pondered how to be compassionate toward this difficult child and yet distanced enough to preserve my own sense of well-being. Finally, I beseeched God, "*You* do it. I can't figure out a way." Then the phrase "ministry of availability" popped into my mind. For some reason, having a expression to pivot around helped me find ways to impersonally love Paige through prayer and simply being available if she ever wanted to talk or needed anything.

Happily, there are exceptions when a new stepmother and a child hit it off immediately and love is effortless. Upon meeting her for the first time, Jeanne's stepson, Joel, exclaimed, "Oh boy, you must be Jeanne!" It was love and warmth at first sight and those feelings continue to this day. In disconcerting contrast, Joel's siblings "were not able to receive the kind of love energy I could give," Jeanne explained. Jeanne never became close to those three stepchildren, although they all came to call her Mom.

For some of our stepchildren, having us available to provide care and safety when they're in dire need will be the greatest of plenty. For other kids, benign neglect works magic. Still others will be tickled to death to accept anything and everything we have to offer.

In reality, there is no magical formula that determines how close stepfamily relations will become. We might all coalesce into one big, happy, "blended" family, or we may need to choose compassionate detachment as our best option for befriending our stepchildren.

COMPLEMENTARY MOTHERING

There can never be too much caring in this world. As far as mothering and stepmothering are concerned, our kids' ability to absorb love will match and surpass our ability to give it. As much as mothers and fathers might like to provide their children with every iota of guidance, attention, and affection they need, it simply isn't possible. Like it or not, there are things—both concrete and elusive—we can't give our children, lessons we're not equipped to teach them, ideas we wouldn't even think to expose them to, and facets of their creativity and passion that we might never draw from them. That being the case, how wonderful for a child when he or she is surrounded by many adults—an extended family of mentors and models—who, through their different viewpoints and skills, can and will augment the children's lives through complementary love, support, and education.

Ideally, stepfamilies can become the village it takes to raise a child, and stepmothers can take on the role of complementary mothers. Complementary mothers are women who expand their stepchildren's lives simply through their own uniqueness and willingness to befriend children who are not their own and engage in the children's lives in a meaningful, heartful, and hospitable way.

Speaking with Heather, the stepmother of two daughters to whom I referred earlier, was an insightful and eye-opening experience. A spiritual seeker and artist, Heather said, "I tried to fill in for the girl's mom in the spiritual and art areas since those subjects didn't interest her—sort of to fill in the gaps without overstepping my bounds." Wanting to find a balance and not cause their mother discomfort, Heather decided upon the direct approach. "I talked to my stepdaughters' mom and told her what I wanted to do and asked how she felt about it. She gave me her permission to 'go for it' in the spiritual and art departments.

"When the girls visited, Carla and I talked endlessly about spiritual issues, values, and experiences, and Kisa and I did art projects together. It was great." In essence, Heather took on the joyful task of complementary mothering. Imagine how she felt when Carla became an ordained minister and Kisa pursued art as a career. Having Heather's interests and talents to complement their own mother's areas of expertise gave both girls a wider base of support and instruction.

When Carla was struggling with a terminal illness, Heather once again became the complementary mother

Kisa needed. As can easily happen when buried under the emotional avalanche of major illness, Carla thoughtlessly said things that hurt Kisa's feelings. Not wanting to add to her own mother's pain, Kisa talked, instead, with Heather about her wounded feelings. As a stepmother, with a tiny open and objective space within her heart, Heather could be totally present to Kisa, understand her feelings, help her come to grips with them, and work toward forgiving both herself and her sister.

I was heartened to hear several stepmothers talking about the relationships they are building between themselves and the mothers of their stepchildren as well as between themselves and the stepmothers of their own children. Grinning broadly, Torie, a thirty-something stepmother/mother, said, "I'm so proud of myself, Sue. I decided that I didn't want an adversarial relationship with either my stepkids' mom or my kids' stepmom, so I asked each one of them out to lunch." With a laugh, she added, "Separately, not together." According to Torie, both lunches began a little awkwardly but ended with the realization that all of the women were actually glad to have a "care-buddy" with whom to share stories, experiences, and advice about all of the children involved.

Unlike Torie, we may not enjoy the luxury of a relationship with our stepchildren's mother that allows us to talk about the part we can play in their lives. But with foresight and intuition, we can usually figure out what is appropriate, helpful, and complementary. Another wise stepmother, Trudie, told me, "My main role as a stepmother was to facilitate a good relationship between the kids and their father and mother." She continued, "I also knew I was important in their lives. In fact, Abbie, the youngest, worships me. Children respect those they learn from and those who care for them."

As mothers, we need to get over our fear that our kids will love us less if they relate well to their stepmother and realize that another caring woman in their lives may enrich them immeasurably. When we can do that, our children will reap the benefits of embracing a complementary mother, guilt-free. As stepmothers, we need to accept that we are not the real mother but that we can choose to befriend and care for our stepchildren to the best of our ability. This will allow more love to flow into our hearts and souls and will give the kids a chance to glean the goodies only we have to offer.

As a step toward becoming a complementary mother, ask yourself, "What if I were not in these kids' lives? What can I bring to them in terms of personality, talents, attitudes, and beliefs that might make them happier and more well-adjusted people?" All of us have valuable contributions we can make to life in general and to our children and stepchildren, in particular. As we open our hearts and offer our gifts to them, our lives and relationships can become richer.

Mentor by Modeling

It can be helpful to do a realistic and gentle inventory of the qualities and attributes you have that may enhance your kids and stepkids' lives. How would you like to express these qualities and attributes? Or, better yet, how can you model them by the way you live your own life?

Lily, for instance, valued physical affection. She shared that neither her stepchildren nor their father were at all demonstrative when they combined forces with Lily and her two children. "I'm a touchy-feely ex-hippie," she said, laughingly. "My kids and I were accustomed to hugging and kissing all the time and laying around with our heads in each others' laps. We were kinda like a basket of puppies, and I think we freaked my husband and his kids out at first, because we were always trying to cuddle with them."

How did it all turn out? With a flip of her hand, Lily said, "Oh, we wore 'em down! We knew we would. It was just a matter of time. Now all six of us are high on the huggy scale."

Ellen, a therapist and communication expert, shared that she made it a point to admit her mistakes to her stepchildren, because they had learned to blame others rather than accept responsibility for their own actions. "I would always say to them, 'I'm sorry. I made a mistake about thus and so, and I apologize.' Then when they did something wrong, I could refer to my apology and tell them, 'It's okay to make mistakes, but you need to admit them and then make amends like I did the other day about thus and so, remember?'"

Ellen added, "I also invited them to be more open about their feelings and ideas by questioning them. Like, I might say, 'Help me understand what you mean by that. I don't think I get it yet.' And then I model speaking about feelings in order to clarify. Just yesterday, I said to my youngest stepdaughter, 'I feel confused by what you just said. Can you put it another way?' When she did, I said, 'I feel hurt by that but also glad that you helped me through my confusion.'"

While not all of us are as cool-headed or as experienced in communication as Ellen is, we can admit our mistakes and model appropriate behavior. We can nonjudgmentally clarify issues and questions with the kids in order to come to a better understanding. Constructively sharing our feelings with all our kids helps them acknowledge their own feelings and learn positive ways to express them.

What do you want to offer to your own children and stepchildren? How might you complement their lives—and probably your own as well—by consciously and naturally modeling your strengths? Focus on what you wish to embrace and enhance, and then model that behavior, for that which we concentrate on, we imbue with power. By doing so we effectively befriend and mentor the youngsters in our lives. Who we are and what we do on a daily basis far surpasses anything we say.

We embrace and befriend the children in our lives in many ways: opening our hearts, welcoming them into our lives with hospitality, modeling authenticity, and offering the precious gift of complementary mothering. We give much but don't always know if what we've given has been received or, sometimes, if it was even worth giving. But if you doubt your influence, consider the lighthearted old saying, "If you think you are too small to be effective, you've never been in bed with a mosquito."

Calming The Churning Waters

Life shrinks or expands according to one's courage.

–ANAIS NIN

Combining families means that "them thar waters is gonna git churned up a good bit." It's something like what I imagine would happen when a mountain stream is stocked with fish. In my mind's eye, I see a truck backing up to the rocky water's edge. In the back of the truck is a big tank filled with fingerling trout. Workers open the tank, dump the trout into the stream, and—chaos! The water churns as the traumatized trout scurry this way and that, seeking a safe haven in their strange new habitat.

While my internal movie may be a little more dramatic than the reality of some stepmothers' lives, it illustrates the large-scale chaos that can occur when families combine. Though few people relish chaos, it is a part of life and often, at least at the beginning, a big part of stepfamily life. But there are ways to courageously cope with the chaos, calm the churning waters, and survive and thrive in challenging times.

GUTS ARE GREAT ADVISORS

When we face a crisis, we often tap into a vast reservoir of intuitive knowing, of gut feelings, that we may not pay enough attention to as a general rule. In times of confusion and chaos, it's advisable to retreat and become quiet. When we become quiet, we can look into the depths of our hearts—just as we would look into an unruffled mountain lake—for the intuitive guidance that is there. Sometimes the waters of our spirits are churned and murky, and it is difficult to tap the reservoirs of our innate wisdom and knowledge. But the waters will settle as we do. Quietly and gently encourage yourself to go inside. Clarity will come.

Maddie was a ranger in Rocky Mountain National Park for several years before she married Max, who had custody of his six-year-old son and nine-year-old daughter. "I was used to running into wild animals in my work, but that did nothing to prepare me for living with Max's kids," she exclaimed. "There were times when I thought it would be easier to face a rabid mountain lion than it was to be in the same house with those kids."

Maddie's situation was complicated by the fact that her stepchildren's alcoholic mother lived four blocks away. It was not unusual for the mother to end up on their doorstep in the wee hours of the morning alternately sobbing morosely to "see her babies" and yelling hysterical obscenities about Maddie. "I came from a family where people hardly spoke above a whisper," Maddie said. "For a while I was so shocked and intimidated by the kids' wacky mom that I did nothing, even though I felt I was losing my mind. Max got a restraining order and that helped somewhat, but one day I simply announced to him and the kids that I was going to the mountains and wasn't sure when I'd be back.

"I went to my favorite out-of-the-way lookout spot in Rocky Mountain Park and sat there for hours. At first I was just numb and then I began to have this sense about what needed to happen." Maddie smiled and said, "When I got home, I was calm and I outlined what I thought we needed to do, which included selling the house and moving out of the neighborhood."

That was four years ago. Today the family lives about ten miles from their old house, and the kids have mellowed considerably. "We have a lot of fun and laughs together. They're still wild animals, but they're more *my* wild animals now," she grinned.

As stepmothers, we all need energy, empowerment, and spiritual support. Often our best guidance is right there inside of us. As we learn to listen to and trust our gut feelings, our intuition becomes much more accessible to us. It is a resource we can draw on as we face the sometimes chaotic realities of daily life. In truth, when we learn to listen well, our guts are our greatest advisors!

Neutralizing The Hassles

Sorting out acceptable parameters and instilling responsible habits in stepfamilies usually includes a period of resistance and hassle from the kids. If children are not accustomed to accepting responsibility for either chores or behavior, they're likely to rebel against what they see as unreasonable demands made by you, the wicked stepmother. And the older the kids, the more difficult the transition—unless, by some miracle, they are longing to please you.

Things have changed since ours was mainly an agrarian society where children were routinely expected to work in the fields and kitchens to contribute to the family's income and survival. Today, in fact, some parents fail to assign their children any responsibilities whatsoever and do everything for them, a mistake detrimental to both child and family. Children feel better about themselves and closer to their families when they are taught to accept certain duties and obligations for the family as a whole. These obligations include respect, kindness, and helping out.

For instance, children gently guided from an early age to assume responsibility for their own messes have a much better chance of developing into responsible and helpful older children. But, as stepmothers, we rarely have the luxury of knowing, let alone training, our stepchildren from an early age. We may luck out and inherit kids who are polite, neat, and well trained, but chances are some training will be required for us to operate comfortably in our homes.

Parent and Stepparent as Powerful Partners

In her highly recommended book, *Parachutes for Parents*, Bobbie Sandoz states, "[I]t's critical that the child's natural parent be willing to provide clear yet loving boundaries for the child and discipline him whenever necessary, since it would be premature for a new stepparent who has not yet established a friendship with the child to do so. The management of boundaries is essential to the success of a positive relationship between the child and his new stepparent, as it offers the child a united front between his natural parent and new stepparent."[1]

Her advice is absolutely right; it's in everyone's best interest when stepparents can get acquainted with their stepchildren in a leisurely and nondemanding fashion, building up trust and affection over time. But most of us live at such a fast pace these days, that taking time is almost an indulgence. Many couples meet their mate, move in together, and merge their families so quickly that it makes everyone's head spin.

Candy and Tim are a good example. "As I look back on it," Candy reflects, "I don't know what we were thinking. Well, obviously we *weren't* thinking. Three weeks after we met, Tim had moved in with me and my three kids. His two kids began alternating weeks with us and their mom immediately." What followed was a chaotic period of adjustment for everyone. "We almost called it quits many times," Candy told me ruefully. The only thing that saved them, she believes, was individual and family therapy.

"The therapists gave us all permission to be utterly confused. Without judgment, they helped Tim and me see that we'd put everyone under pressure by jumping right into living together, and they gave the kids permission to vent some of their frustration without alienating anyone." With a sigh, she said, "The main thing the therapists taught Tim and me to do was become a united front. They helped us learn to be a partnership, something we desperately needed, 'cause otherwise it was five against two."

How Stepfamilies Work—or Don't Work

The wisdom of the partnership advice Candy and Tim received from their therapists is backed up in a recently released study by Dr. James Bray, a clinical psychologist at Baylor College of Medicine in Houston. Bray's nine-year study found three types of stepfamilies: romantic, matriarchal, and neotraditional.

Romantic. In the romantic-type stepfamily, both partners hope for instant love between stepparents and kids. "They have difficulty realizing that stepfamilies differ from traditional nuclear families and children need time to get to know stepparents," Bray states. Romantic couples are the most divorce-prone.

Matriarchal. In the matriarchal-type stepfamily, the couple marries primarily to be with each other. The wife has custody of children from her previous marriage and wants full charge of raising them and running the household. "Problems with this arrangement tend to arise when the couple conceive a child of their own," Bray says. "The husband then wants to get more involved in parenting, which can cause conflict within the couple because the wife is used to being in charge."

Neotraditional. "Neotraditional couples seem to work best of the three types of stepfamilies and seem happiest," Bray said. "The husband and wife view the stepfamily as a partnership. They manage the household as partners, and allow at least a year for the stepparent to be accepted in a parental role."

Bray found that some romantic and matriarchal stepfamilies survived by changing their expectations over time. "Parenting is the No.1 stressor in stepfamilies," he stated. Although his study concentrated on stepfather families, the types of families he outlined are equally applicable for stepmothers.[2]

To our chagrin, Gene and I agree that we fell into the romantic category during our early years together. We are among those who survived by eventually maturing into a neotraditional stepfamily, a powerful partnership equally concerned and committed to ourselves, each other, and all of our adult "kids." It was a colossal upper when my unmarried son, Brett, said recently, "Mom, you and Gene are my shining example that marriage can work, that two people can be happy together."

Forming a compassionate and powerful partnership with your mate is one of the best ways to assure your own peace of mind and the success of your marriage. As a bonus, children surrounded by the secure structure of a partnership stepfamily are given a strong foundation for their natural developmental process.

To help develop strong partnerships, I suggest that you and your mate talk candidly about your type of relationship and how you might want to alter it. Reading informative and supportive books together or separately can provide valuable insights and instructions. These activities may stimulate important conversations between you and your husband, inspiring and encouraging you to change anything that needs changing. Of course, as you well know by now, I believe therapy is also a helpful tool.

Facing Power Struggles with Kids Together

We've talked about power struggles before, but, because they are such a challenge in stepfamilies, it's worth looking at them again. Nowhere in stepparenting is it more important for a couple to be united and empowered partners than in the midst of power struggles between themselves and the children.

Power struggles between parent and child are, we need to remember, between adults and children. Children are given into our care, not the other way around. As adults with many years experience and accumulated wisdom, we have both the inner and outer resources to shoulder the responsibility and caretaking duties for the children in our homes. It stands to reason, then, that we also have the authority and obligation to make age-appropriate decisions and choices for the kids while they are under age and in our care.

It's altogether natural for children to push against parental limits and lobby for privileges before they are mature enough to make wise and thoughtful choices. Families who work through such confrontations in constructive ways provide valuable experience for the both children and adults. The key to constructive solutions lies in the partnership between stepmom and natural father.

Deprived of a true partnership with their mate, it's easy for some stepmothers to capitulate to untimely and inappropriate demands from children out of a desire to be loved and accepted. Others can be overly strict with their stepchildren because they fear being manipulated, don't like the child, or feel resentful about having to take responsibility for them.

Sylvia had never been married when she inherited three fairly out-of-control stepchildren. Her friends adamantly voiced their doubts that she had the patience or practicality to raise these kids whose father, unfortunately, had simply plunked them in her lap with the understanding that they were now her responsibility. As a very accomplished career woman, Sylvia set out to prove that she could "succeed" at mothering. Sylvia shared a regret, "If I had it to do over again, I'd be less harsh with my three stepkids. But at that time, I really wanted to 'whip them into shape' to please my husband and prove to everyone else that I could be a good mother."

I danced on the opposite side of the coin in my insecure, wanting-to-be-loved years, prone to acquiesce to almost anything the girls asked for. Both Sylvia and my responses were based in fear: Sylvia's fear of failure and my fear of rejection.

Where do you fall on the power-struggle continuum? How do you respond to your stepchildren's demands? Can you and your husband discuss emotionally intense issues and come to an agreement with each other? Are you, personally, able to remain grown-up and make wise decisions about what you intuitively know is right in this particular instance or for this particular child? Or do you vacillate and waver under the pressure that the kids bring to bear? If you're normal, like me you've probably been both wise and waffly.

Basically, kids need parents and stepparents who are strong and decisive, ones who listen to what the children have to say, consider different options for circumstances and individual maturity, and are fair in their decisions and discipline. Each child, of course, is different. Some are mature enough at age twelve to be marvelously responsible baby-sitters while others are still act like babies themselves at that age. Children are reassured when we know and care for them and make decisions according to their individual capabilities.

Although kids may push and tug against adult edicts, their sense of security rests on knowing that there are adults whom they can count on, adults who respect them but resist their attempts to do more than they are capable of developmentally. It's good to remember that what the kids say they want and need may, in actuality, not be what they secretly wish for. Kids want and need the security provided by parental figures who can say "no" to inappropriate requests; they do not need more power and control than is appropriate.

In essence, it's best when a couple can become empowered parental partners and deal with struggles that arise with the kids together, or at least in accord with one another. Children need the security that a parental unit provides, and we need the sanity togetherness insures.

The Chore Wars

Chores rank among the most popular battlefields upon which we struggle for power and supremacy with our kids. Since, in my own eyes, I absolutely do not qualify as an expert in the field of training willing helpers, I refer you once again to Bobbie Sandoz's book, *Parachutes for Parents,* which I think is unsurpassed in its practicality concerning this and many other areas of child rearing.

In the chore department, I learned from Bobbie the art of providing choices and limiting freedoms when poor choices are made. After years of teeth gnashing, hair tearing, and lose-lose power struggles, Gene and I finally hit upon a simple strategy that might also win the chore wars in your home.

Every Saturday morning we compiled a chore list and left it on the kitchen counter with instructions for each child to choose one or two chores, depending on the length of the list and the difficulty of the chore. Obviously, the early birds took the choicest chores. But the choice was theirs: sleep or choose first. The sleepyheads sometimes got creative, set their alarms, sneaked down, signed up, and went back to bed. When that happened you can imagine the screams of protest from those who were used to getting up first and having first choice.

Only after the kids had completed their chores that day were they free to pursue their personal activities. A few exceptions were made. For instance, if Brett had a soccer game on Saturday morning, he was allowed to go to the game but had to come right home afterward and finish his chores before going off with his buddies to do other things. Of course there were some times when the rules were bent, but we usually followed the prescribed format pretty well and turned a deaf ear to most protests. After a period of adjustment, the chore list totally neutralized the hassle and arguments that had always accompanied division of labor before. What a relief.

Tofu versus Junk Food

While every family is different and will come up with their own solutions, stepfamilies are "mixed marriages" in the truest sense of the term and, as such, often need to blend totally different cultures as they look for their own creative solutions to classic family hassles.

"I had a hard time remembering that my stepdaughter was used to a different culture than mine," Susan said. "She was raised on sugar and sandwiches, and I favored health food and exercise. The poor kid practically starved the first few months she lived with us." How did it all shake out? I asked. "My husband and I agreed that Molly could eat anything she bought and cooked for herself, but if she didn't have her own food, she ate ours." With a smile, Susan added, "Molly got used to eating our stuff, but she really pigged out when she visited her mother and usually came back on a junk food high."

With her husband's full support, Susan responded to her stepdaughter's differing epicurean culture by adopting the when-in-Rome-eat-what-the-Romans-eat philosophy. How great it would be if we stepmoms could learn to step back a bit and view our stepchildren's different background and training as an up close opportunity for cultural study—sort of an in-house anthropology class. Viewed from that impersonal yet interested vantage point, we can often more easily tolerate, understand, and even enjoy the various styles and practices introduced by our stepkids.

Defusing the Discipline Dilemma

For some of us "discipline" conjures up unpleasant images of parochial school, rulers on wrists, withdrawn affection, ridicule, abusive parents, and who knows what all. In spite of the fact that my parents were wonderful and well-meaning people, as a little girl discipline and withdrawal of love became synonymous in my mind. Not surprisingly, as an adult, I was a reluctant disciplinarian. In order to be an effective parent, I desperately needed to defuse the discipline dilemma by reframing the concept as a positive one.

In my delvings, I discovered that the original philosophy of discipline was, in fact, deeply nurturing. The word "disciple" is rooted in the Latin word for "learner," *discipulus*, which suggests that a teacher, guide, or coach is involved wherever discipline is needed.

Conditioned to expect that love would be withdrawn when I was disciplined, I needed to retrain myself to see discipline as a fair and equitable teaching tool, not a pejorative term for some controlling punishment. As a young, struggling single mom, I learned about "natural and logical consequences" and tried—sometimes successfully, and sometimes not so successfully—to link that idea with discipline and to act as I imagined a loving and trustworthy teacher, guide, or mentor would.

The more I remained in my "role" of teacher and mentor and sustained a compassionately detached attitude, the more cooperative my boys were. Correspondingly, as soon as I got hooked into thinking it was my fault they were misbehaving or descended into a guilty sense that these children had been ruined by my divorce, the boys became ornery and uncooperative.

These lessons learned as a single mom helped prepared me for the role of stepmom. Often vulnerable and confused, we stepmoms are likely to feel personally attacked, overly responsible, or rejected when our stepkids act out. In reality, we often are the target of their acting out behavior which makes it exceedingly difficult to maintain an impersonal and neutral attitude.

But, life runs more smoothly when we can train ourselves to discipline from a compassionately detached place within ourselves. For it seems that "natural and logical consequences" go both ways. Dispassionately and calmly disciplining using natural and logical consequences elicits a favorable response from children and stepchildren, but on the other hand, when we are emotionally and personally attached to the kids' behavior, discipline can turn into punishment.

A wonderful way to defuse the discipline dilemma and remain compassionately detached is to invite the kids to decide for themselves about the consequences for unacceptable behaviors. I remember one conversation centered on asking Mike and Brett, "What do you think is a reasonable consequence for sneaking into the liquor cabinet and drinking some of the liquor?" With great chagrin, the boys came up with consequences that both Gene and I considered excessive. The boys' willingness to be hard on themselves put us in the wonderful position of graciously and benevolently meting out clemency. Among the four of us, we agreed on a long-forgotten consequence and working together toward it was very powerful and unifying.

When administered fairly and with understanding and a sense of cooperation, external discipline ideally matures into a personalized, self-motivated set of checks and balances. Given a chance to develop organically and naturally, self-discipline gradually emerges as an internal desire to maintain order, balance, and harmony with one's self and with others.

Accentuate the Positive

Accentuating the positive may not totally eliminate the negative, as the old song has it, but it does encourage the positive to grow and flourish and puts the negative in perspective. As stated earlier, energy flows where attention goes. Therefore, if we want to neutralize hassles and calm churning waters, it's best to focus on those actions and attitudes that we want to see continued. Attention and recognition are big rewards for people, no matter what their age. As the saying goes, "That upon which the light of attention is shone becomes more visible. That which is focused upon is magnified."

Looking back, I cringe remembering the negative attention we gave the kids and all rules we had for them: Don't sit on the arms of the couch; don't eat in the living room; don't chew loudly; don't, don't, don't. This old accentuate-the-negative attitude was brought home to me just the other day when Paige perched on the arm of the couch and then jumped up saying, "Ooops, I shouldn't sit here, should I?" My tight-jawed inflexibility around all our rules flashed through my memory as the new me—actually the older, mellower, who-cares-about-couches-or-what-*they*-think me—shrugged and said reassuringly, "*I* do."

Of course, some rules are necessary and prudent, but focusing solely on what is wrong with a person or situation and what shouldn't be done accentuates the negative and, completely overlooks the positive. It's amazing how many discipline dilemmas can be resolved by focusing on the positive and downplaying the negative. Would that I had known that sooner.

From the wisdom of hindsight, I now know it's much easier to calm the churning family waters, neutralize emotional and power struggle hassles, and defuse the discipline dilemma when we accentuate the positive. Even while running a relatively tight ship, we can still adopt a spacious, accepting, and adventurous attitude, one that eventually can make family life fascinating and delightful.

Encountering Ordinary Chaos

All families—whether natural or step—brim with ordinary or normal chaos. My friend Diana once told me during a discussion about grandchildren, "I have sort of loose standards for normal." It's healthy to have fluid and movable standards for normal where kids are concerned, and it would probably do many of us good to relax our standards a bit. I know Diana's flexibility has been a big factor in helping her retain her equilibrium and good humor throughout some disquieting family ups and downs.

Clinging to rigid standards usually brings us tight jaws and uptight family members. How much better if we adopted William James's approach to wisdom, "The art of being wise is the art of knowing what to overlook."[3]

When chaos erupts in your family, as it's sure to, pause before reacting. Ask yourself if the tumult is natural kid stuff that you would be wise to overlook. If so, turn a deaf ear, if your can. If not, intervene as needed.

Just What Is "Quiet"?

As a general rule, normal boys are like bear cubs wrestling in the forest. They naturally create a cacophony of noise as they casually smash into walls and crash on the furniture. Girls, on the other hand, usually stir up more emotional and psychic turmoil while also doing their fair share of squealing and screaming. In short, kids are just plain loud and thrash about a good bit. With the right attitude, it's easy to see those traits as part of their innocent charm.

Of course, if you need quiet because you have a migraine, an important deadline to meet, or simply because you're fed up with noise and pandemonium, it's totally okay to set limits by saying something like, "I know you guys are just playing, but I don't feel well and need you to be quiet right now." Setting limits and sticking to them is fine: it's equally important to let the kids know they're not being "bad" but rather that you simply need quiet. There's a good chance that a child's definition of quiet and yours will differ and you may need to spell out your needs, "I need you to play in the backyard away from the bedroom" or "It would be better if you all went to your rooms or to a friend's house right now."

In order to understand what was over-lookable, Sophia, who had no children of her own said, "I had to find a group for stepmoms, because I didn't have any experience with kids. Many of the things I saw as problems and obsessed over, my group showed me were just normal every day children stuff." She continued, "I gotta tell you that news was not overly welcome. I thought 'Oh, my God, if this is normal, what will I do if we get into *abnormal*?' I felt overwhelmed for a while, but I calmed down and learned to accept more stuff as time passed."

Early-visit or After-visit Rebellion

Because it's so prevalent, I want to reassure you that it's natural for kids to experience a period of adjustment when they change homes temporarily, whether they are returning from a visit with their other parent or coming to visit you. It's best not to reward any acting-out behavior with undue attention. Getting hooked into the "let me see if I can make it all better" trap or taking their actions as a personal affront is not only detrimental; it also perpetuates the behavior. Calmly going about your business and casually offering hugs and your presence, gently accepts the fact that transition times are tough for kids.

You and your husband may need to agree on action to be taken about post-visit rebellion and have each parent discipline his or her own children, especially in the first year or so of "blending." If a child's behavior is unacceptable, one natural and logical solution is for his or her parent to gently but firmly remove the child from the family for a while, explaining, "I can see that it's hard for you to be here right now. That's okay, but it does mean that you're choosing to be away from the family for a little bit. Would you like me to sit with you in your room [or on your bed, or whatever is this child's place in your home] for a few minutes? If not, would you prefer the door to the room open or closed?" Such gentle but firm discipline allows children to realize they have a choice about their behavior and also lets them see that they are accepted even when their behavior is not.

When we know that it is difficult for a child or teenager to make the transition from home to home and family to family, it's relatively easy to remain calm. Wisely recognizing that his or her behavior usually has nothing to do with us, personally, definitely makes us happier stepmothers.

FACING EXTRAORDINARY CHAOS

It's not always easy to distinguish ordinary from extraordinary chaos. It is helpful when the distinction can be made, however, because we often need to respond differently to extraordinary chaos and/or seek additional support. While it's impossible for this book to touch on all aspects of the extraordinary chaos that we might encounter in our merged families, I want to highlight a few that many stepmoms experience.

Our Inner Terror

First, let's look at our own inner terror—that internal chaos or excruciating anxiety that sometimes accompanies remarriage and stepmothering. Facing marriage or remarriage and stepmothering can cause our own unresolved issues to rise to the surface. Unhealed wounds may threaten to overwhelm us. Kids are usually amazingly good at sensing feelings of weakness, and, especially if they're ambivalent about having a stepmother, may exacerbate your vulnerability by skillfully pushing all of your "hot" buttons. Don't fall into the trap of either blaming yourself or feeling victimized, but simply hie yourself off to someone who can help you sort through your feelings and transform your terrors.

Ironically, the terror you feel may be a clever method your soul is using to help you transform feelings that have outlived their usefulness. When that is the case, your stepchildren act as valuable catalysts in your own healing process. Painful as it can be for a while, you may eventually be thankful for their help.

Overly Needy Children

Children who are not receiving enough love and attention from their natural parents may see a stepmother as a life raft, the answer to an unspoken prayer. If you are genuinely eager and excited about accepting that task from this particular child and can embrace the role of surrogate mother with wisdom and enthusiasm, everyone wins. For most of us, however, it's not that simple. Just as most stepchildren need time to figure out how they feel about us, stepmoms also need time to allow relationships between ourselves and the kids to evolve of their own accord.

Emma's stepdaughter began calling her "Mom" before Emma and the girl's father were even married. "It took me by surprise when she called me Mom the first time, and I didn't say anything," Emma said. "But it didn't feel right to me. I didn't want to be called Mom. I'm not her mom. In fact, I'm nobody's mother and that's just fine with me." As gently as possible, she let her stepdaughter know that she preferred to be called Emma.

Calling Emma, whom she barely knew, "Mom" was an indication of the little girl's neediness. The only daughter of a distant father and disinterested mother, Alison was starving for attention and affection and hoped that Emma would provide them. But Emma is a very busy career woman and, although she cares for and about Alison, is not inclined to take on the primary mother role—nor should she be expected to.

If you become the stepmom of a needy child who looks to you as a mother substitute, it's crucial that you know how much you're willing to be involved in this child's life. Without clarity, you might find yourself more deeply committed than you feel comfortable with and more involved than you can handle. Agreeing to do or be something for someone that you don't want to do or be only leads to resentment, disappointment, and pain for both of you.

Naturally, feelings can change and there may come a day when there's nothing you'd rather do than throw your arms and heart open to that child and embrace whatever complementary role they desire from you.

Unless or until you're sure you want to assume a major mothering role, don't do it. And if you decide that an intense involvement is not for you, the tricky part will be not feeling guilty. Please let guilt go, if possible, and give yourself credit for honoring your limits and boundaries. Guilt closes your heart to yourself. A closed heart cannot form healthy relationships with anyone.

Dealing with Teenagers

The teenage years often cause us the most consternation. Not only do kids have more freedom and, consequently, are given more opportunities to make poor decisions, they're sometimes defiant and limit-pushing to boot. But, since some of that behavior is natural and expected, we can take heart from talking to other parents and lovingly holding the necessary lines.

But what happens when teen behavior pushes beyond normal limits? Sometimes the struggle inherent in extraordinary crisis bonds us more closely to our mate. Such was the case with Maude and Ralph. In junior high, Maude's son spent a rough year running with the wrong crowd, dabbling in drugs, and perfecting the art of lying. Through it all, Ralph supported Maude and intervened with his stepson at times when a strong hand was needed. As soon as Mick, Maude's son, had cleaned up his act, Ralph's daughter, Penny, began similar behavior.

Slapping her hand to her forehead, Maude said, "Not again!" She continued, talking of the effect of the experience on her relationship with Ralph: "In a way, going through such similar experiences helped us empathize with each other and realize that we'd gotten through it once and, by golly, we'd darn well get through it again." With a wink, she said, "It was a relief for me to no longer be the only parent with a 'difficult' kid."

Ceaseless trauma and conflict caused by such things as consistent drinking, drugs, or other destructive behavior from a family member place a tremendous strain on families. Ravaged by the constant stress, families and marriages become vulnerable to collapse unless they receive the outside help and support they desperately need. Unfortunately, part of the problem often lies in not recognizing the need for help. If your stepfamily is racked by any sort of extraordinary stress and pain, find help and support immediately. Friends and relatives can often provide excellent personal support systems. Check the phone book for your local Mental Health Department or Alcoholics Anonymous and call them. They can give you a good idea about available resources. Seeking support in times of extreme chaos is not weakness, as some would have us believe. Rather, it is wisdom. None of us need to go through turbulent times alone. There are many guides and helpers, seen and unseen, human and ethereal, who are glad to be of assistance.

While difficult, maintaining a positive attitude in times of extraordinary chaos is important. Realistically, few people can sustain an elevated attitude all the time.

It's natural for our moods to fluctuate, especially in times of crisis, but usually, with a little internal nudging and external support, most of us can regain a positive and optimistic outlook.

The bottom line, however, is that your family's most important resources are you and your husband. Working together as a united pair, the two of you can have a powerful effect on the family as a whole, and on acting-out children in particular. Two heads and two hearts joined in a single purpose are definitely better and more effective than one.

Meeting Crisis Hand in Hand

At no time does a couple need to be clearer about their commitment toward each other than in times of crisis. Crisis calls for each of us to be our mate's very best friend. A Swedish proverb says, "Shared joy is double joy, and shared sorrow is half-sorrow." As a grim reminder that crisis can tear us apart if we're not closely united, many marriages break up after the death of a child or during a life-threatening illness. Such break ups occur partly because men and women respond to crises differently and, when they most need each other, their differences tend to make them feel the most alone.

For instance, men are often trained to stifle their feelings while women feel freer to express theirs. Women usually have many women friends with whom they can share their sorrow, but men rarely have such close companionship. Men have been taught to "keep a stiff upper lip," whereas women have more permission from society to "fall apart" or take a tragedy "very badly." Though many of us are embarrassed to cry in public, women are less likely than men to be labeled weak when tears flow.

When our hearts are broken, it isn't easy to open them to another in unconditional love and acceptance. But that's exactly what we need to do if we are to be close to our mate during crisis. During my years as a psychotherapist and hospice worker, I've known many couples who forged unbreakable bonds by being lovingly and unconditionally present for each other during crisis. Although it often wasn't easy, they accepted their differences in dealing with the pain and refused to be distanced and alienated from each other. When it was appropriate, they sought help for themselves and their marriage.

As an example, Jeanne and Les faced the trauma of his sixteen-year-old son's cancer hand-in-hand. "Sometimes, when we felt the most alone and alienated from each other and from Sean, our son, one of us would reach for the other's hand merely as a physical symbol of togetherness," Jeanne said. Throughout the two years of treatment and turmoil with both Sean and his biological mother, Jeanne and Les steadfastly plugged away at keeping their communication open and heartful. "We were so drained of energy most of the time that all we could do was fall in a heap at the end of the day, but we made sure that we fell in a heap together and that we didn't leave feelings undiscussed for very long," she said.

After successful treatment Sean, now in his early thirties, is living and cancer-free. Both Jeanne and Les feel that the crisis deepened their friendship and love for each other as well as all of the children in their combined family. "Looking back, it was a trip through the bowels of hell, but it turned out to be good for all of us," Jeanne said.

⚜

Courageously facing the inevitable hassles of life together as a stepfamily is the first step toward neutralizing or resolving them. Though we often don't realize it at the time, we grow our souls in the midst of chaos. Crisis and turmoil can reveal both our authentic self and our true heartfulness, both of which help us remain sanguine and calm in the face of small hassles and crucial confrontations alike. As we face the churning waters of stepfamily life openly, we begin to experience the calm that comes with trusting our own knowing and acknowledging our own wisdom. When we willingly embrace the pain, the joy, and the chaos—both ordinary and extraordinary—we begin to recognize the true strength within and among us as individuals, sacred partners, and families. Together we can survive—and thrive.

PART SIX

Gathering The Gifts

Whatever their outcome, the profound relationships in our lives give us the riches of loving. That wealth is the only wealth that means anything in the end.

—MARION WOODMAN

The most precious gift to be gathered from the stepmother journey is expanding our ability to give and receive love. Our soul's growth is immeasurably enriched by alternately stumbling and soaring through the ever-changing aspects of accepting someone else's children into our hearts.

In essence, we are in this life to become adept at sharing the gift of love. In her early eighties my friend, Annabelle, says, "The wonderful thing about age is that you don't regret love. Love is the only thing that really lasts." That sentiment was echoed repeatedly by the stepmoms I talked with.

No matter how much trauma and pain accompanied it, not one woman I spoke with regretted the love she gave or accepted as a stepmother. Those few stepmoms who, to date, have gathered nothing but grief from their stepchildren are still thankful for the experience and hopeful that good feelings might be on the horizon. In their own way, each shared that the journey itself, no matter how demanding, was helping them become better, more compassionate people.

It's easy to love those who love us back, or to shower attention upon naturally lovable babies and endearing puppies. It's not so simple to make the *choice* to love. But, as Mary Ann Evans—whose pen name as a novelist was George Eliot—pointed out, "The strongest principle of growth lies in human choice."[1] Choice is one of the most powerful gifts we have been given. How we use it increases or limits our capacity to love and expands or diminishes our souls. Usually the more difficult the choice, the greater the soul's growth.

I am the first to admit that looking back on active stepmothering years is sometimes more fun than actually being in them. But isn't that the case with all the worthwhile challenges we accept—career, marriage, motherhood, and self-realization? Life is a learn-as-you-go endeavor, which means we almost always do a lot more muddling through than sailing effortlessly along, especially when attempting to master a new role such as stepmothering.

But hang in there, make loving choices, trust yourself, hold hands with your beloved, and lean on others in your support system. Along the way are many precious gifts and the riches of love to be gathered from becoming and being a mother-by-marriage.

The Blessings of Blending

Love is a fruit in season at all times, and within reach of
every hand. Anyone may gather it and no limit is set.

—MOTHER THERESA

For many of us, the hard work of blending two disparate
family units into one eventually yields a harvest of blessings: more people to love, more ways in which to grow,
and, in my case, the chance to mother girls as well as
boys. It's important for all stepmoms to realize that these
blessings do not arrive automatically but are the results
of much tilling, fertilizing, praying, and patience.

To their eternal credit, each stepmother I interviewed
seemed to feel that, no matter how infertile the soil or
how few the flowers, she was nearer her own and God's
heart as a result of being planted in a stepfamily. Even
those women whose marriages ended in divorce affirmed
that living in a stepfamily provided abundant insights
into their own strengths and vulnerabilities, and were,
therefore, welcomed greenhouses for soul growth.

Personally, my life today is greatly enriched because of
my relationship with Gene, Lynnie, and Paige. That doesn't
mean that I didn't shake my fist at The Divine often and
mutter disgruntledly, "How can I 'bloom where I'm
planted' when the damn place is so arid and unfriendly

right now?" However, the metaphorical weeds our family yanked and the locust infestations we wrestled with along the way make every blossom and butterfly in our current relationships all the more precious.

As with all gardens, our stepfamily gardens demand a lot of work but can bloom prolifically when tended carefully. Though the growing season may be long and arduous, eventually there is usually a harvest of blessings.

Sowing Seeds of Love

Like it or not, the traditional "garden variety" family is changing. Combined families are quickly replacing families of origin, and, if statistical predictions are correct, stepfamilies will soon be in the majority.[1]

Whether we are weekend or live-in stepmoms, or rarely see our stepchildren, those of us "blending" families are gardeners. We hold the responsibility and privilege of nurturing and nourishing the fragile buds of our society's emerging hybrid family. From a stepfamily born out of loss, we are challenged to build a viable and supportive extended family. Ideally, we will become the village it takes to raise a child while nurturing ourselves in the process. In reality, all of us—women, men, and children—thrive better when surrounded by a caring village community.

As a shining example of the village concept, stepmom Ruth said, "I asked my stepchildren's mother how she felt about my relating to them, and she answered, 'They can use all the adult friends they can get.'" The biological mother's Solomon-like concern for her children's well-being is all the more admirable because they live continents apart. To help her stepsons' mother feel more a part of the family, Ruth keeps her up to date on the boys' lives via e-mail. Stories of compassionate cooperation such as this give me hope that our emerging hybrid families have great possibilities for being healthy and happy havens for all concerned.

As women, I believe we are uniquely suited to creating a healthy climate in which we, our own children, and our inherited families can grow and flourish. The hard part is sustaining and maintaining a secure environment that gently encourages all to bloom. From the depths of my heart, I believe that we can cultivate and grow such nurturing families.

To gather the gifts of a stepfamily garden, we must continually choose to sow and resow the seeds of love. Each tiny seed we sow, every compassionate choice we make, brings us, and those near to us, greater connection, love, and peace of mind rather than alienation and anxiety.

Stepfamilies offer the possibility of increased love and laughter as well as the probability of soul growth. However, the requirements of such family-gardening include sinking our hearts into the very ground of our being and mucking our hands around in the roots of our family trees to unearth those hidden beliefs and half-buried attitudes that continually trip us up. We'll also be called upon to apply liberal doses of fertilizer to the fragile new growth of relationships that sprout up within our combined family circles. Not to worry about finding fertilizer—there's usually more than enough readily available in the first few years of family merging!

Circles of Love and Influence

Besides personal growth, a medley of other blessings and gifts can be ours once our stepfamily is deeply and securely rooted. One of the sweetest is surely the opportunity to expand our intimate circles of love and influence.

Circles, the form used for many religious rites and spiritual gatherings, are sacred. The sanctity of the circle is found in nature and spiritual life. Mother Nature uses circles as a major element in her profuse earthly garden and within our vast universe. Mother Earth, Father Sun, and Grandmother Moon are round as well. We also speak of those we love as our family "circle," whether they're related by birth, inherited, acquired, or chosen as kin.

A sacred circle of love knows no bounds. Realizing that our circle of love has positively influenced our families—especially our stepchildren—can make our hearts absolutely sing. Recently Gene and I received a thank you card from Sallie, a young woman friend of my stepdaughter, Lynnie. We had given her an audio tape of mine in hopes of bringing her some comfort as she grieved for her stillborn son. Sallie's note said, "Must let you know how wonderful Lynne has been with all of her support. As I listened to your tape, I did hear a lot of 'Lynne' in all that she says and is!" It was indeed an upper to learn that a friend of Lynnie's sees a similarity between us.

With one natural son and one stepdaughter, Margaret, of whom I've spoken earlier, said, "Just having a girl around has been a joy for me. Having an opportunity to share some of my life with her has been a real blessing." I'm sure that Margaret is also a blessing to her stepdaughter and I especially appreciated one poignant story she shared: "An important part of my life has been the woman's circle I've belonged to for many years. When Stacy's first period came, my group created a ceremony for her to celebrate this new phase of her womanhood." I asked about Stacy's natural mother's reaction to her daughter participating in such a ritual and Margaret answered, "Oh, she was included. The mom was an integral part of the ceremony." This is another instance of creative and complementary mothering as both women come together to enhance a child's life experience.

Pondering the Blessings of Blending

I invite you to pause here a moment and ponder what blessings you are giving and receiving in the sacred circle of your family. Whose heart are you soothing, and how is your own being touched? What seeds are germinating within your soul? What gifts will inevitably flower? When we're feeling drained, exhausted, or discouraged, quietly taking a peek at our inner blessing-barometer can lift our hearts.

In bestowing and accepting the "blessings of blending," we create stronger, wider, and deeper spheres of love and influence within our families and also within the collective human family. What we do for our own naturally affects the many.

Growing From Stepmother to Heart-Mother

The role of stepmother carries a vast potential for opening our hearts, broadening our vision, and increasing the scope of our awareness. In fact, each person intimately welcomed into our lives opens a world within us that would otherwise remained closed. We are changed, honed, and influenced by every individual who touches our hearts. Every relationship in which we invest time and emotion has the potential for illuminating facets of ourselves otherwise shrouded in mystery and secrecy. And therein lies a profound blessing—the possibility of growing from stepmother to heart-mother to the children marriage brought into our lives.

Before I could refer to my stepdaughters as my heart-daughters I needed to grow comfortable with the name. I needed to mature, and the girls and I needed time together, experiences shared, actions forgiven, and reality accepted before I could honestly be a heart-mother. For me it means that these two young women whom I mothered—but to whom I will never be mother—live within my heart every bit as much as my sons do. In the depths of my soul, I have grown to become Paige and Lynnie's heart-mother.

In no way do I see my self-designation impinging upon their natural mother's place in their hearts, souls, and lives. Her place is secure for she is their mother, not I. But I have mothered, mentored, and befriended both girls. My spiritual mother, Annabelle's wonderful phrase— "Born of my heart, our bloodline is spirit"—describes the bonds between Lynnie, Paige, and myself, bonds that I treasure as incredible—and hard-earned—blessings.

I was extremely touched by the stepmothers I spoke with because each, in her own way, shared a willingness to open her heart to her husband's children. Naturally, many stepmoms were overwhelmed when first accepting the role but, nonetheless, all seemed to have a deep and heartfelt desire to embrace and welcome their stepchildren. I'm not naive enough to believe there are no "wicked" stepmothers out there. However, more or less consciously, most stepmothers realize that inherited children offer them opportunities for soul-growth and provide them with tangible ways to usher more love into their own lives and into the world.

Granted, the blessings gathered from soul-growth and spreading love are often more easily seen from the wise perspective of hindsight than while trudging through the trenches. I remember a moment when I got a peek at my own soul perspective. I was having a difficult day with Paige when I met my dear friend, Bonnie, for lunch at our usual restaurant. Patiently, she listened as I sobbed and blurted out my pain (and undoubtedly cemented our reputation as really weird women with this particular restaurant). There was no doubt in my mind that Bonnie understood and empathized with my woes, so her question surprised me. "Can you love her, anyway?" she asked. My immediate "Yes" surprised me even more than her question had. In her best therapist manner, Bonnie continued, "And what does that tell you about yourself?" "That I'm a damned, masochistic saint!" I blurted out. Whereupon we dissolved into gales of laughter as the other lunch patrons doubled their efforts to ignore us.

That tear-and-laughter-laced lunch was a turning point for me, a spontaneous realization about just how dedicated I was to the personal and soul-growth involved in our stepfamily dynamics. I was bound and determined to love to the best of my ability, even if it meant many years of loving in a compassionately detached way with Paige.

To show you how far we've come in our healing and connecting, Paige and I will soon travel together to swim with my beloved free dolphins. Inviting her to join me in such a personal and sacred adventure would have been unthinkable a few years ago. Now it's something we're both looking forward to with great anticipation. To me, my present bond with Paige is an affirmation that miracles do bless us when we manage to keep our hearts open. As I struggled to grow from stepmother to heart-mother, I tried to remember that, whether born of my body or delivered by marriage, my children's souls and mine are made of the same stuff.

GLEANING THE GOOD STUFF

My son Brett inadvertently gave me a wonderful gift recently when he laughingly said, "Our family puts the 'fun' in dysfunctional!" It's true. Although we have areas of dysfunction just like every family, step and nuclear alike, we also share a lot of laughter, fun, and support. Brett made me ponder how wonderfully healthy it would be if we could lighten up our attitudes toward family dysfunction and concentrate, instead, on gleaning the good stuff from our fertile family circles.

What might some of the good stuff be? Of course, each family's good stuff will be different, but I noticed several recurrent themes running through the lives of the step-moms I spoke with that corresponded with my own experience. As you read ours, I hope you'll realize your own unique good stuff.

More People to Care About

Although I've mentioned this before, it bears repeating. Truly the best blessing of blending—the 'goodest' stuff, if you will—is the opportunity to love and relate intimately with more people. And the circle just keeps expanding. When asked the blessings her adult stepsons brought to her life, Gwen answered, "Oh, I have an angel of a daughter-in-law and three almost grown grandchildren who enrich my life greatly."

Belinda, who had a rough first few years with her stepdaughter, said, "It was so great to go to Katie's house and see that she has pictures of *all* the family up in her Rogue's Gallery." "Even you?" I asked jokingly. "Yep, even me, the Wicked Stepmother. Quite a distance we've come, eh?"

Creating Broader Vistas

As part of a merged family, both adults and children are given the opportunity to see many differing personalities and souls at work and play. As a result, new doors of consciousness and awareness are opened within all of us. Many women realized how their own vistas had been broadened by intimately interacting with kids "from a different world," as one stepmom put it. By their very uniqueness, our stepchildren mirror differing aspects of ourselves to us than do our natural children. Sometimes that's heavenly, sometimes it's hellish, but it's almost always growthful.

Many women I talked with shared how wonderful and broadening it was to have their husband's influence for their own children. I am very thankful that my sons have had Gene as a model, because he is totally different from their father. Because of their two very different father/male role models, Mike and Brett have a more panoramic view of masculinity and what it means to be a man. Of course, they will continually create and recreate their own maleness, but having been parented by two very dissimilar men, gives them a deeper well of experience and insight to draw from.

The Wonder of Grandchildren

Ah, yummy. Now these little people are definitely good stuff! All seasoned stepmoms, including myself, placed grandchildren high on their lists of blessings.

I know that for those of you now parenting live-in children, the idea of *more* children—especially the ones that indicate you're getting older—may not be very appealing. Twenty years ago I'm sure I would have needed a hefty swig of an antacid if anyone mentioned the idea that a greater number of grandchildren were among the inevitable "blessings" of our blended family. Today, however, I'm a pretty typical "grammy"—besotted, amused, filled with awe, and head over heels in love with our little guy—and, I might add, vastly relieved that I'm not the parent.

Learning to Muddle Through

Confession time. No. On second thought, I have absolutely no desire to remember, let alone list, all the unexpected and unwanted things we muddled through in the course of active stepparenting. Those memories deserve to fade away, just like the recollections of labor pains dim with time. Suffice it to say that I could have lived nicely never knowing that bail bondsmen were open twenty-four hours a day or experiencing the mess that four dogs, four kids, and a cat can create all at once.

Muddling through the unexpected and undesirable were often unwanted experiences that forced Gene and me into some semblance of understanding and tolerance. And many of those calamities were bonding experiences for the kids that now provide them with fodder for great bouts of dinner table hilarity. Thankfully, our adult kids sometimes say, "I think we better 'take it outside' and spare The Units [Gene and me] this particular bit of trivia." You betcha! While firmly believing that all the lessons we learned were beneficial to our overall soul-growth, I'd just as soon remain ignorant of the ones I was graciously spared.

The Gift of Levity

Levity lightens all loads. I have a fantasy that our guardian angels are continually tickling us with their feathers, whispering encouragements, "Wonderful woman, laugh...Lighten up...Look for the humor...Let the tears of delight and humor flow ... Dance ... Sing ... Find joy in it all ... "

It is my sincere belief that the more a mom or step-mom can *en*joy, the more her entire family circle will live *in* joy.

✦

While I wish I'd learned to gather the gifts, be grateful for the blessings, and concentrate on the good stuff earlier in the process of cultivating our hybrid family circle, I believe that I did the best I could considering who I was at the time. Most veteran stepmoms agree that it is an incredible blessing to be more relaxed women now; women who regularly remember to count our blessings and glean the good stuff as it comes.

Stepping-Stones On The Spiritual Path

Darest thou now O soul,
Walk out with me toward the unknown region,
Where neither ground is for the feet nor any
path to follow?

—WALT WHITMAN

Women who have the courage to embark upon the path of stepmotherhood are, indeed, walking toward an "unknown region," as Walt Whitman writes. Each of us will be challenged to find our place; to create the "ground" for our feet and the right "path to follow" as we bring our combined family circle into being. Those of us who have said "yes" to marriage and stepparenting, probably see relationship as a valuable spiritual path. For us, intimate relationships are—or can become—a sacred part of our journey toward reunion with the Divine.

Being aware that our intimate relationships are part of the spiritual path helps us remember that we and our family are bound together in one of the most sacred relationships we can experience. We must be gentle with this precious relationship, mindful and careful of it, reverent toward it. Family bonds are at once infinitely strong and profoundly fragile. They can be broken. Given our vulnerability, at birth each of us deserves to receive a beautiful label: "Precious and Fragile. Handle with Care and Compassion."

MEANING AND PURPOSE IN LIFE

Our journey toward the Divine is intimately connected with meaning and purpose in life. What gives meaning and purpose to your life? What makes you love the person in the mirror? What gives you the courage and wisdom to walk through the dark valley of despair? What gives you hope? What lights the creative fires within you? What fills you with joy and brings peace of mind?

Sages, philosophers, and spiritual leaders have struggled with these questions for centuries, just as we grapple with them in the wee hours of the morning. Our answers to ourselves will come as love notes, or "soul nudges," from our deepest being. Each individual's soul nudges will vary.

And, if you're reading this book, my guess is that relationships bring meaning and purpose into your life, and that the more supportive and loving they are, the happier and more fulfilled you feel. If so, relationships are stepping-stones on the spiritual path for you, as they are for me.

Deep within my heart, I cherish the belief that we, our mates, our children and stepchildren come together to devote ourselves to each other, ministering to each other's souls in subtle and overt ways. And, of course, parenting of any kind requires devoting ourselves to the well-being of smaller and weaker ones given into our care. Our intimate relationships provide us with daily opportunities for choosing to be as loving, kind, and gentle as possible. Relationships also bring us pain. But as we face and overcome these inner and outer obstacles, our souls are honed and our hearts opened.

Any spiritual path, because it is part of life itself, joins daily joys with daily griefs. Such is life—the paradox of light and dark, good and evil, soft and hard, simple and complicated. Such are relationships—heart-wrenching as well as heart-lifting. And, therein, lies our growth.

WALKING THE SPIRITUAL PATH

I love the old adage, "Don't be so spiritually minded that you're no earthly good." To me, it's a wonderful reminder that the spiritual path is strewn with reality—the situations, choices, and actions that need our attention each day. We, as stepmoms, have chosen to do some of our "earthly good" in a blended family. How we *are* and how we *act* in the most minuscule day-to-day endeavors strongly affects the universal quality of our life and the life of our chosen family.

Each time we meet an irksome problem with compassion, understanding, and acceptance, or lovingly embrace another person with grace and joy, we take a step along the spiritual path. In the course of a typical stepmom's day, there are numerous opportunities to transform the difficult into the divine, the mundane into the holy. I wish I'd realized this fully when all the kids were living at home. Envisioning this sacred transformation would have been a deep comfort then, as it is now that I've become older and wiser.

Images that concretely express this ongoing transformation of the difficult into the divine encourage us and give us hope. Vivian, a wise young stepmother, finds the image of stars effective. "I imagine that each time I handle something well—and sometimes I handle it by handing the kids over to their dad—but that's better than murder, don't you think?" she asked with a grin. "Anyway, each time I handle a situation or a screaming kid in ways I consider pretty cool, I say, 'Okay, God, there's another star for my crown,' and I throw a star up to heaven." When things get really difficult for Vivian, she sits on her deck and looks up at the stars. Gazing at the stars reassures her that she is being watched over and supported by a loving God and that her struggles and successes are not going unnoticed.

It doesn't matter how we visualize transforming the difficult aspects of stepmotherhood into sacred steps along the spiritual path. It only matters that we *do* find ways, as one dear friend puts it, to "kick it upstairs."

Kiln of Kinship

To be strong, useful, and retain its beauty, pottery is placed in a kiln. The intense heat of the kiln fires pottery to its optimum strength and burns away impurities, making it more resistant to breaking. Only after being subjected to the inferno of a kiln is the beauty, depth, and color of glazed pottery revealed. It doesn't take a big imaginative jump to realize that our intimate relationships create a similar kiln in which we, too, are strengthened and tempered, and our impurities consumed to reveal the beautiful and unique nature of our souls.

In the kiln of kinship, no part of us remains unchanged—and the changes are almost always for the better. Holding the vision that our relationships are a sacred part of the spiritual path, we know they bring opportunities for strengthening and refining us. Without such an evolutionary philosophy, it's difficult to discover the growth within the kiln of kinship. Even with that understanding, pain is pain and, therefore, tempting to avoid. But when we close ourselves off from experiencing the full range of emotion—from deep joy to deep pain—we are less than we can be.

As Kahlil Gibran beautifully suggests in *The Prophet*, I find great solace in the thought that God, the Potter, anoints the cup bearing my pain with His own sacred tears. From the wisdom of age and experience, I'm also aware that much, if not all, of my stepmother pain was self-chosen, not on a conscious, human level but at a soul level. And the growth from it has been profound.

Because I was addicted to approval, appreciation, and obvious signs of lovability, stepmothering was a painful soul-stretcher. Simply choosing to be a "good woman," doing what was necessary, and giving what was desirable without hope of much credit or too many outward signs of acknowledgement was tough. Transforming my fantasy relationship into an appropriate one between the girls and me was difficult. But eventually doing so became a tempering and purifying process, one that has allowed a cozy and supportive love to grow between us, a wonderful bonus for which I'm deeply grateful.

As we move through our stepmother journey, there will be days when we wonder if we can survive the fiery intensity of the kiln of kinship, and other days when we're warmed to the core by those we love and those we are still trying to love. Such feelings are typical. Most stepmoms vacillate on a continuum from feeling inflamed, enraged, and frustrated to sharing warm-fuzzies and heart-melting closeness. The intense range of feelings appears to be an integral part of the spiritual path.

To help maintain your equilibrium within the kiln of kinship, pause, ponder, and choose before you act or speak. Breathe deeply, talk with a supportive friend, give thanks for all that happens around and within you, and remember—*please* remember—to treat yourself with consistent gentle kindness.

Gifts Gathered On Our Way

Spiritual gifts are often paradoxical, such as strength coming through weakness or wisdom coming from mistakes. The stepmothering path offers us many of these spiritual gifts. Let's look at a few of them now.

Self-Awareness

In the nitty-gritty of daily family life, each stepmom is given the gift of facing her fears, vulnerabilities, and insecurities. I say this is a gift, because each fear transformed is a freedom gained, each vulnerability acknowledged is a step toward more authenticity, and each insecurity healed means an increase in self-confidence. Each day a stepmother is invited to be truly herself through sharing her deepest wisdom and most unique talents with those she loves. That self-awareness is a gift to her, her family, and the world as well.

Love

Our hearts are the rivers through which God's love flows. As we free ourselves from the fears that dam our ability to love, our hearts open and love flows freely to us and to others. Love yourself first, for only then do you truly have love to give.

As we realize and reclaim the genuine bond between woman and child, no matter whose blood runs through their veins, we can become complementary heart-mothers who are able to hold our stepchildren in gentle, compassionate hands and, in return, be enjoyed and respected as true mentors and friends. Whatever the problem, love is the answer.

Forgiveness and Compassion

As compassionate women, we can empathize with others and weave into the very fabric of our being a gentle knowledge about their wounds and their wonder. Forgiveness grows naturally out of such intimate awareness and understanding. Our challenge is to be as compassionate and forgiving with ourselves as we are with others.

For me, writing *The Courage to Be a Stepmom* has been an exercise in forgiving myself. Revisiting actions and attitudes, and the reasons behind them, has enriched my understanding of the woman I was and the wounds with which I was struggling as I tried, without much outside support, to create a family from our mixed brood. Also, talking with all of our four kids was an eye-opener. They didn't even remember many of the things I'd beaten myself up about for years! For two reasons, tears trickle down my face as I write these words. First, I feel sad about how hard I was on my younger, stepmother self—how much I "shoulded" on her. Second, I'm so thankful that my actions and attitudes didn't hurt the kids as much as I feared they might.

So, please remember: Even if you do quite a lot wrong, things can still turn out all right. When our hearts are in the right place—at least a majority of the time—even the most awkward stepmuddling can eventually yield "good stuff," such as understanding and closeness.

Lack of forgiveness toward ourselves and toward others blocks the flow between us and our Source, whereas, the ability to forgive allows love, laughter, and creativity to flow to and from us. Beyond our harsh judgment of ourselves and of others, the Divine waits for us with an ever-flowing font of forgiveness. I invite you to meet me there.

Patience

At age twenty-seven, I met my spiritual mother, Annabelle, whom I mentioned earlier. Annabelle is a gifted intuitive and transformational therapist. One of the first things she gently told me was, "Darling, you have *no* patience whatsoever. Therefore, we'll pray that you are willing to be willing to be patient." Although being patient sounded like it would be restful, I had little hope of attaining such a goal.

Over the years, my prayer changed from "Please help me be willing to be willing to be patient" to "Please help me find patience within me." Today I can truthfully say I am pretty patient for an Aries. That's quite a miracle of persistence—and yes!—patience. Nowhere has patience been more welcome than in my stepmothering role.

Acceptance

Everything in life that we really accept undergoes a change. Sometimes the change is subtle and easily missed. Other times it hits us right smack in the face. Of course, there are unacceptable actions and intolerable attitudes. However, it's best for all concerned when we can forbid the unacceptable action or attitude but wholeheartedly accept the person.

Melody's stepson, for instance, delighted in teasing his younger half-brother. At her wit's end, Melody sought out therapy to learn to set limits and follow through with natural and logical consequences with her stepson. However, the first thing the therapist helped Melody do was stop blaming herself and work on accepting both herself and her stepson. Accepting herself as she was at the moment actually helped Melody grow a firmer backbone, and, in the wake of her transformation, her stepson's behavior eventually improved also.

When the need for acceptance comes up, breathe deeply and relax. Move into your heart and send compassion to yourself and the situation. Ask yourself these questions: What is important right now? What do I need to do in order to move closer to an attitude of acceptance? Listen deeply for a reply from your wise inner Self.

Gratitude

With gratitude, our hearts soften and peace of mind becomes a constant companion. An effective and simple gratitude "exercise" is this: Make a conscious effort to be grateful for waking up to a new day. Pick one thing about each family member, including yourself, for which you can be thankful today. Some days you may be especially grateful to one of your stepchildren for teaching you how to enhance your patience and self-control. Other days you may simply be grateful that you made it through the day. Gratitude is indeed a pearl of great price, and it is also a sweet shortcut back to Spirit.

Trust

One of our most sacred gifts is the ability to trust ourselves, our wisdom, and our innate goodness. So many stepmoms revealed that trusting themselves and their intuition is a difficult and ongoing task.

The inability to trust ourselves, others, and life in general *is* difficult. As women, we have been taught not to value our own perceptions and insights. Living in a world dominated by logical, linear thinking—one that values mind over spirit and intuition—diminishes our trust in what we know. If you start questioning yourself, find another woman with whom you can talk honestly about your perceptions, understandings, and insights. Women, together in a spirit of approval and support, can help each other learn to trust themselves.

Silent Service

In order to feel worthwhile, each of us needs to love and to be of service to others. Yet for many stepmothers, much of their service is silent and receives little recognition or outward reward. Because our egos are not often fed nor our fabulous gene pools applauded, caring for stepchildren provides our spirits with beautiful opportunities to give simply for the joy of service.

This doesn't mean that you become a slave or that you "suffer in silence" by becoming a martyr. Not at all. It does mean, however, that you keep your expectations realistic and welcome occasions for honing your soul through silent, openhearted service without the expectation of reward. Because most stepmothers will get the chance to serve silently, we might as well use our serving as a spiritual practice. Silent service, transformed through love and spiritual focus, leads us inward and outward toward the person we are destined to become, our highest and best self.

These are just a few of the gifts that can be gathered along the spiritual path of stepmotherhood. Savor and celebrate them, for they will serve you well as you travel through the valleys and mountains of life on your journey to the Divine.

A MOUNTAIN PARABLE

Imagine that someone you care deeply about invites you on a hike. At first, things go well, but that quickly changes. The difficulty of the trail looming before you shocks and intimidates you. What you had envisioned as a comfy and companionable walk turns into an arduous trek filled with discomfort and discouragement. But you resolutely put one hiking boot in front of the other, drink lots of water, rest when needed, ask for help when the trail becomes too tough to navigate alone, and take your time. Eventually you reach the top. Although the climb wearied you to the bone, the view from the summit is awe inspiring, invigorating, and enlivening. The hard hike was worth all the effort.

After much cheering and high-fiving, you and your companion glance down at the difficult trail you've just climbed. "Wow! How'd we do that?!" you exclaim, and then look up again to enjoy the view. Overflowing with a sense of accomplishment, love and gratitude pour effortlessly from your heart. Drinking in the beauty and splendor of nature at her most majestic, your soul soars. Never have you felt so in tune with yourself, your companion, and the Creator. Never have you felt so blessed or so free. And the best part? It's all downhill from here.

Similar feelings of exhilaration filled me when our nest emptied and all the kids were on their own. In a sense, I felt I had *grown* my way up to the top of

Stepmother Mountain. Having been singed and seared, my soul deserved to rest amid the wildflowers and vistas of this welcome peak.

Of course in real life, it's never "all downhill from here," but we do have times when we seem to glide effortlessly through life and are "in the flow." Early empty nest was one of those intervals for me. It's wonderful to give ourselves permission to enjoy the top-of-the-mountain, flowing times, because inevitably another lesson will come along, and it's up the hill we go yet again.

Our reward at the top of each mountain is a wider and more expansive perspective—a soul's eye view—as well as the ability to recognize a higher purpose woven into the tapestry of our lives and loves. At the end of any conscious journey, the questions are simple: "Did I do the best I could?" and, more importantly, "Did I love well?" Each challenge successfully met deepens our awareness of our inner strength and allows us to gather the joys and rewards from that which may once have been steeped in sorrow. Such is the sacred path of step-motherhood.

If you are struggling up the steep path of active step-mothering, please take heart from those of us who now have a view from the top of Stepmother Mountain. Here we can see the many gifts to be gathered along the path, gifts that can last a lifetime. Among them are an increased ability to share love, soul-growth, grace, gratitude—and more grandchildren! All are blessings we can cherish forever.

Ascending Stepmother Mountain invites us to be fully present in our lives and conscious of our journey, to grow our souls and open our hearts while taking gentle care of ourselves and the family given into our keeping. Although it's not easy, it *is* possible, and the rewards can be infinite.

Stepmother Emeritus

I feel somewhat like the Little Blue Engine in Watty Piper's classic children's story, *The Little Engine That Could*. After years of going puff, puff, chug, chug and repeating, "I think I can—I think I can—I think I can," I've reached the top of Stepmother Mountain. Now chugging steadily along the Stepmother Emeritus tracks, I can smile and say, "I thought I could. I thought I could. I thought I could."

During the climb when I was dispirited and the "I think I cans" became very weak, some inner or outer boost always brought back hope, enthusiasm, and a willingness to start chugging back up the mountain. My dad sometimes called me a "cockeyed optimist" and that may be true. I resonate with the idea that we can get optimism from the Earth itself. I feel that as long as Mother Earth can make a spring every year, so can I. As you know from reading this book, there were wintery times during my active stepmothering years, times when spring seemed a figment of my imagination. But the cockeyed, naive, optimistic part of me always came back to life and our family continually experienced spring after spring, no matter how hard the winters had been.

Although I can take partial credit for the fact that the six of us eventually created a truly blended family, we were all in this together. If any one of us had flat out declared, "I want no part of this," there would have been nothing I could have done. Together, we worked hard, we loved to the best of our ability, we were lucky, and we're all grateful for the life we now share.

At this writing, Gene and I live in Boulder, Colorado. Paige, Brett, Mike, Lynnie and her husband, Shawn, and our grandson, Josh, all live within an hour's drive. They are wonderful, caring, successful people who are each chugging up the various mountains of young adulthood. We love them, feel incredibly blessed to be close to them—both geographically and emotionally—and we are proud of each and every one.

If I had it to do over again, I would go more slowly with the girls, let go of unrealistic expectations, be more honest with Gene, set better boundaries, lighten up and laugh more, and definitely take everything less personally and less seriously. In other words, I'd do it like my fifty-eight-year-old self, not my thirty-four-year-old self. Or put another way, I *couldn't* have done it differently unless I'd been much better prepared with education, counseling, and a large dose of realism-training. I simply did the best I could with what I knew and who I was at the time.

My bet is that your heart is in the right place and you're doing the best you can also. Please, if you're feeling overwhelmed, treat yourself with gentleness and kindness and find others who can instruct and guide you. Winter will pass, spring *will* come. Since I did it, I know you can—I know you can—I know you can—I know you can—I know you can!

Twenty Guidelines for Stepmoms

1. *Go slowly. Give yourself and the kids time ... and then more time.*

Allow yourself—and the kids—time to find your unique place within the family circle. Ooze into the sometimes chilly waters of stepmothering slowly and carefully, one tentative little toe at a time.

2. *Love and care for yourself first, for only then do you truly have love and compassion to give.*

Take time out to rejuvenate and ruminate. Give yourself permission to rest and enjoy the solitude it takes to stay connected to your own unique inner core.

3. *Live gently with yourself and others.*

We learn, grow, and love more readily when coaxed forward by compassion and understanding than we do when bludgeoned by self-recrimination and judgment.

4. *Seek out the guidance and support you need.*

It is incredibly wise to seek out those people, groups, and situations in which you can be supported and listened to. We all deserve to be tutored and tenderly cared for as we muddle through the hard times and sail through the joyous ones.

5. *Nurture your relationship with your husband.*

After caring for yourself, caring for your marriage is the most important thing you can do. After the children are grown and have lives of their own, you and your husband will be together. In order for that togetherness to be rewarding, your friendship needs to be nourished along the way.

6. *Give yourself credit.*

Acknowledge your efforts, learn from your mistakes, and celebrate your successes. Give yourself gold stars.

7. *Trust yourself and your intuition.*

Remind yourself that you are wonderfully wise in the art of relationship and quietly access and acknowledge that wisdom at all times.

8. *Let go of unrealistic expectations.*

The adjustment period for a stepfamily usually takes years rather than weeks or months. Expecting instant-family, affection, and/or acceptance sets us up for instant and continuous disappointments. It's great to have a positive attitude but few specific expectations.

9. *Expect and accept only respect.*

Respect for each individual member of a family is a non-negotiable.

10. *Set and honor realistic limits and boundaries.*

Choose your battles wisely, and then stick firmly to those limits that are important to your peace of mind and sense of well-being.

11. *Communicate clearly and truthfully from your heart.*

It is through communication that we reveal ourselves to others. Through words and actions we are unveiled and, thereby, able to appreciate and value one another.

12. *Listen intently with the goal of understanding.*

Listening in order to more fully understand ourselves and another is one of the most precious gifts we can bestow.

13. *Remember that most members of a stepfamily have grief to heal.*

Because stepfamilies are families born of loss, members (including ourselves) are vulnerable and need time, tenderness, and understanding in order to heal.

14. *Try not to take things too personally.*

A vast majority of the time *you* are not the real target of the slings and arrows flung in your direction. A wise stepmom learns to duck and dodge.

15. *Embrace stepmothering as a spiritual path.*

Choosing to embrace and care for another's child/children can open our hearts, grow our souls, and add meaning and purpose to our lives.

16. *Never say anything derogatory about your children's or stepchildren's natural parents.*

It's perfectly okay to be a sounding board if the kids need to grump about one of their parents but never wise to agree with them or criticize a natural parent.

17. *Treat each child with kindness, courtesy, and respect.*

The only real requirement of you as a stepmom is to be kind and respectful to your spouse's children.

18. *Kids are kids—accept and enjoy them for who they really are.*

Children are wonderful and blessed beings who can bring untold joy into our lives. But they can also be irritating, demanding, and frustrating as the dickens. Expecting kids to be miniature, civilized adults is unrealistic and futile.

19. *Relax. Lighten up. Laugh.*

When we can relax, we invite the process of blending a family to unfold in its own time and way. The more flexible and adventuresome we are, the more thoroughly we'll enjoy all aspects of stepmothering/muddling.

20. *Hang in there!*

Almost every stepmother emeritus I know advises, "Hang in there, it's all worth it in the end!"

Notes

THREE STRIKES BEFORE YOU START

1. Census Bureau data cited by the Stepfamily Foundation, Inc. on the World Wide Web at www.stepfamily.org. Click on "statistics."

2. John Anyto, *Dictionary of Word Origins* (New York: Arcade Publishing, 1990), 501.

3. See Stepmothers International, Inc. on the World Wide Web at www.stepmothers.org.

TAKING IT ONE "STEP" AT A TIME

1. "A Servant to Servants," in *The Poetry of Robert Frost,* ed. Edward Connery Lathem (New York: Holt, Rinehart, and Winston, 1969), 64.

2. Beverly Potter, *The Worrywart's Companion: Twenty-one Ways to Soothe Yourself and Worry Smart* (Berkeley, CA: Wildcat Canyon Press, 1997), 3.

3. *Sunbeams: A Book of Quotations*, ed. Sy Safransky (Berkeley, CA: North Atlantic Books, 1990), 38.

BEING A TRUE FRIEND TO YOURSELF

1. May Sarton, *Mrs. Stevens Hears the Mermaids Singing* (New York: W.W. Norton, 1965), 172. *Hamlet* 1.3.52-63.

SETTING (AND STICKING TO) LIMITS AND BOUNDARIES

1. Maya Angelou, *Gather Together in My Name* (New York: Random House, 1974), preface.

Marriage Is For Good Friends

1. Kahlil Gibran, *The Prophet* (New York: Alfred A. Knopf, 1951), 16, 15.

1. May Sarton, *Journal of a Solitude* (New York: W.W. Norton, 1973), 109.

2. The Perils of Pauline—a silent film episodic serial from 1914 with 20 chapters. Starred Pearl White and Crane Wilbur, directed by Ray Taylor.

Communication Is The Heart Of Marriage

1. *A Course in Miracles—Volume One, Text* (Huntington Square, NY: Foundation for Inner Peace, 1975), 41.

2. Leo Buscaglia, *Wise Words: Perennial Wisdom from the New Dimensions Radio Series* (Carlsbad, CA: Hay House, Inc., 1997), n.p.

The Heart Of The Matter

1. Joan Evelyn Ames, *Mastery: Interviews with Thirty Remarkable People* (Portland, OR: Rudra Press, 1997), 189.

Calming The Churning Waters

1. Bobbie Sandoz, *Parachutes for Parents* (Honolulu: Family Works Publications, 1993), Index-119.

2. John Bray and John Kelly, *Stepfamilies: Love, Marriage, and Parenting* (New York: Broadway Books, 1998).

3. William James, *The Principles of Psychology* (New York: Dover Publications, Inc., 1955), 320.

STRENGTHENING YOUR MARRIAGE

1. George Eliot, *Daniel Deronda* (Oxford: Oxford University Press, Inc., 1987), 67.

THE BLESSINGS OF BLENDING

1. The Stepfamily Foundation, Inc. on the World Wide Web at www.stepfamily.org.

Acknowledgements

No book is brought to life without the assistance of countless people, and please know that I appreciate each and every one of you who has helped midwife *The Courage To Be A Stepmom* into existence. A resounding thank you goes to all the stepmothers, stepfathers, and stepchildren who generously shared their stories with me. Gold stars and deep gratitude to my stepdaughter, Paige, who courageously permitted me to be totally honest about our struggles with one another. A thousand thank yous to Julie Bennett, my friend and publisher, who encouraged me to undertake this project and held my hand throughout the process. This book is so much better because of the artful copyediting skills of Jean Blomquist and my friend, Diana Somerville. Thank you both for honing, pruning, and augmenting in such wonderful ways. Thank you to editor Roy M. Carlisle who made valid suggestions and continued to listen to me even when the going got tough. As ever, warm thanks to my husband, Gene, for his unfailingly support during the inevitable highs and lows of the writing process—and for his ability to make me laugh at the most opportune moments.

About the Author

Licensed psychotherapist Sue Patton Thoele lives in Boulder, Colorado, with her husband, Gene. She is a mother and stepmother emeritus whose passions include being with her family, writing, and swimming with free dolphins. Sue is a bestselling author of many books including *The Courage To Be Yourself, The Woman's Book of Courage,* and *Heart Centered Marriage.*

Back cover photo (clockwise from top): Gene Thoele, Sue Thoele, Brett Hall, Lynne (Thoele) Williamson, Paige Thoele, Mike Hall

Wildcat Canyon Press publishes books that embrace such subjects as friendship, spirituality, women's issues, and home and family, all with a focus on self-help and personal growth. Great care is taken to create books that inspire reflection and improve the quality of our lives. Our books invite sharing and are frequently given as gifts.

For a catalog of our publications, please write:

WILDCAT CANYON PRESS
2716 Ninth Street, Berkeley, California 94710
Phone: (510) 848-3600, Fax: (510) 848-1326
Circulus@aol.com